THE BROOKINGS INSTITUTION is an independent organization devoted to nonpartisan research, education, and publication in economics, government, foreign policy, and the social sciences generally. Its principal purposes are to aid in the development of sound public policies and to promote public understanding of issues of national importance.

The institution was founded December 8, 1927, to merge the activities of the Institute for Government Research, founded in 1916, the Institute of Economics, founded in 1922, and the Robert Brookings Graduate School of Economics and Government, founded in 1924.

The general administration of the Institution is the responsibility of a self-perpetuating Board of Trustees. The Trustees are likewise charged with maintaining the independence of the staff and fostering the most favorable conditions for creative research and education. The immediate direction of the policies, program, and staff of the Institution is vested in the President, assisted by the division directors and an advisory council, chosen from the professional staff of the Institution.

In publishing a study, the Institution presents it as a competent treatment of a subject worthy of public consideration. The interpretations and conclusions in such publications are those of the author or authors and do not purport to represent the views of the other staff members, officers, or trustees of the Brookings Institution.

Federal Tax Treatment

of the Family

HAROLD M. GROVES

A background paper prepared for a conference
of experts held April 4-5, 1963, together with
a summary of the conference discussion

Studies of Government Finance

THE BROOKINGS INSTITUTION

WASHINGTON, D.C.

Foreword

The provisions of the federal individual income tax relating to the treatment of the family have an important bearing on the fairness of our tax system. Since the adoption of the income tax in 1913, the federal law has made an allowance for the personal circumstances of the taxpayer through the personal exemption. In 1948, the present $600 per capita exemption, the additional exemptions for the aged and the blind, and income splitting were adopted. In 1954, a deduction of up to $600 was allowed for the expenses of child care incurred by working mothers and by single people. These provisions do not arouse widespread public disapproval or criticism, although many experts contend that they do not provide an entirely rational basis for the tax treatment of the family.

This volume includes a study undertaken by Professor Harold M. Groves to provide background material for a conference on the tax treatment of the family, held at the Brookings Institution on April 4 and 5, 1963, together with a summary of the discussion at the conference. The purpose of the conference was to provide an opportunity for a group of experts to analyze the present provisions and to narrow down the differences of opinion with regard to this significant element of the tax system.

The conference was attended by twenty-seven attorneys and economists from universities, research institutions, government agencies, and private practice, representing various shades of opinion on the tax treatment of the family. The participants were invited in their personal capacities and not as representatives of the organizations with which they are affiliated.

While the author assumes full responsibility for this book, he wishes to acknowledge the generous investment of many others in it. Several doctoral dissertations at the University of Wisconsin—particularly one by Douglas Thorson—laid the groundwork. The original impetus to undertake the project, much assistance at all stages of its development, and guidance through its several drafts came from Joseph A. Pechman. Valuable comments and suggestions were offered by the reading committee, consisting of C. Harry Kahn, Oliver Oldman, and Norman B. Ture, and by Richard Goode, Carl S. Shoup, and Lawrence H. Seltzer. The conferees who assembled to discuss the manuscript are largely responsible for the final chapter, and some of their suggestions were incorporated in the final draft of the other chapters. The calculations and charts are largely the work of Edward Weigner, who assisted the author throughout the project. Mrs. Caroline Nejedlo and Mrs. Dorothy Machigashira typed and retyped the manuscript. Mrs. Virginia Haaga edited the manuscript and prepared the index. The author is thus much indebted to many sources for generous help and participation.

This volume is the fourth Brookings publication in the series of Studies of Government Finance sponsored by the National Committee on Government Finance. The National Committee was established in 1960 by the trustees of the Brookings Institution to supervise a comprehensive program of studies on taxation and government expenditure. The program is supported with funds provided by a grant from the Ford Foundation.

The views expressed in this study are those of the author and of the conference participants and do not purport to represent the views of the National Committee on Government Finance, or the staff members, officers, or trustees of the Brookings Institution.

ROBERT D. CALKINS
President

October 1963
The Brookings Institution
1775 Massachusetts Ave., N.W.
Washington 36, D.C.

Studies of Government Finance

Studies of Government Finance is a special program of research and education in taxation and government expenditures at the federal, state, and local levels. These studies are under the supervision of the National Committee on Government Finance appointed by the Trustees of the Brookings Institution, and are supported by a special grant from the Ford Foundation.

Contents

Tables

Charts

CHAPTER I

Introduction

THE PROBLEMS OF APPLYING the tax system to the family are primarily associated with the individual income tax.[1] This tax is dedicated to the ability to pay doctrine; it is a highly flexible and adaptable instrument and invites refinements to the simple taxation of net income at proportional or graduated rates. As a matter of fact, graduation itself makes necessary a decision concerning the family unit to whose income the schedule of rates shall apply. Should the incomes of single persons and those of families be subjected to the same tax scale, to distinct scales, or to the same scale after dividing the family income into individual portions? Beyond this, many refinements in an elaborate law are efforts to tailor the system to differences in

[1] Except for some incidental attention to other taxes, this study will be confined to the net income tax. It may be noted, however, that the death tax is hardly less permeated with family considerations. The inheritance tax particularly adapts rates and exemptions to the relationship of the heirs to the deceased. And the federal estate and gift tax, while ostensibly basing its single rate schedule on the aggregate of transfers, favors transfers to a surviving spouse (marital deduction). It gives wide application to the philosophy of splitting a tax base between spouses, which will be discussed in some detail in Chapter IV. The sales tax is not readily adapted to family concessions, and indeed its opponents frequently charge that it imposes a penalty on large families. However, the exemption of food from the base of a retail sales tax is said to mitigate this. And proposals have been made for income tax credit for sales taxes paid on a minimum amount of purchases per capita. This, according to some observers, would introduce the equivalent of an income tax exemption into a sales tax model.

family responsibilities.[2] The result is a considerable array of income tax institutions—particularly so-called splitting, exemptions, and certain personal deductions, which are reviewed in this study.

All of these techniques have been the subject of considerable research,[3] and no detailed review of the literature will be attempted here. Rather this study will try to provide a fresh analytical and philosophical treatment, to cover an area usually considered in fragments, and to present as clearly as possible a considerable agenda of problems. It is offered as a basis for discussion rather than a program of action.

The federal tax treatment of the family was last changed in

[2] Historically the idea of making allowance for the fact that persons with equal incomes may have different responsibilities is of later origin than the net income tax itself. It is said to be "an outgrowth of the rising sense of social responsibility and concern for the individual member of the state." (See Paul J. Strayer, *The Taxation of Small Incomes* [Ronald Press, 1930], p. 44.) However, as we shall see, differentiation may be pushed to the point where it is largely self-defeating.

[3] A work on income-tax splitting that is drawn on substantially in this book is an unpublished doctoral dissertation by Douglas Young Thorson ("The Selection of a Tax Unit Under the Income Tax," University of Wisconsin, 1962). Much of the discussion of splitting is in the law journals, but there have been a few brief but good analyses of the equity aspects of the issue in other publications. See, for example: Oliver Oldman and Ralph Temple, "Comparative Analysis of the Taxation of Married Persons," *Stanford Law Review*, Vol. 12 (May 1960), pp. 585–605; Carl Shoup, "Married Couples Compared with Single Persons Under the Income Tax," *Bulletin of the National Tax Association*, Vol. 25 (February 1940), pp. 130–35; William Vickrey, *Agenda for Progressive Taxation* (Ronald Press, 1947), pp. 274–305; Joseph A. Pechman, "Income Splitting," testimony submitted to the House Committee on Ways and Means, *Tax Revision Compendium*, Vol. 1 (November 1959), pp. 473–86. See also U. S. Treasury Department, *The Tax Treatment of Family Income*, reprinted in *Community Property Income*, Hearings before the House Subcommittee on Ways and Means, 80 Cong. 1 sess. (1947), pp. 848–87.

Comments on family tax exemptions pervade the entire literature of public finance. Many views are summarized in Strayer, *op. cit.*, Chap. 3. Authoritative research on the subject has been done by Lawrence H. Seltzer, and the results will soon be published by the National Bureau of Economic Research. The present author has had the benefit of reviewing an early draft of this work. Parts of Seltzer's excellent study have been published in *Tax Revision Compendium* (cited above), pp. 493–514. Other papers in the same volume, particularly those of Wilbur J. Cohen and Eveline M. Burns on the taxation of the aged, are valuable.

The authoritative work on deductions is C. Harry Kahn's *Personal Deductions in the Federal Income Tax* (National Bureau of Economic Research, Princeton University Press, 1960). This work began as a doctoral dissertation at the University of Wisconsin. See also his paper and those of Melvin I. White and Harvey E. Brazer in *Tax Revision Compendium*.

1954, when the $600 deduction was allowed for expenses of child care incurred by low-income working mothers and by single people. In that year the concessions to some single people associated with splitting their incomes under certain conditions were also broadened. In 1948 the present $600 per capita exemption, the additional exemption for the aged and the blind, and income splitting were enacted.

These provisions have not aroused widespread public disapproval or criticism, although Congress is periodically asked to change them in minor detail. A considerable number of critics, however, are firmly convinced that our present tax treatment of the family is irrational and inexpedient. In any case the search for a sound rationale to support what is often taken for granted should be rewarding.

The Issues

Our subject is particularly timely because it is related closely to the much-discussed current issue of broadening the tax base in order to reduce rates to support economic incentives. In some respects and some aspects it is also related to the so-called erosion and corrosion of the tax base. In many cases graduated rates and exclusions are alternative means to the same end, but the implications of the choice between the two need definition. In this chapter these broader aspects of the subject are reviewed.

Underlying all of the specific problems of family taxation are conflicting philosophies of equity in taxation. These also will be briefly reviewed here. Discussed later is the question whether the family differentiations in the statutes really serve to promote the equity objective, which presumably is their end.

An Historical Note

Within the lifetime of many living Americans the income tax has advanced from a mere subject of debate to the mainstay of both the federal and the over-all tax system of the United States. Notwithstanding a late start, the United States, under the pressures of two very expensive wars, has developed this tax to the point where

it is relied on more than in any other country.[4] Thus as the federal
tax celebrates its 50th anniversay in 1963, its proponents can relate
a success story of the first order. These proponents no doubt include
the tax reformers of an earlier day who said that since all taxes come
out of income, the most plausible means of tax distribution is one
based on income. They seem to have done very well at selling their
wares to the American public. All too well, say the dissenters. But
the reformers at least should be satisfied.

However, it seems fair to say that neither the erstwhile reformers,
who are disposed to favor the direct taxation of income, nor the
critics, who are disposed against it, are very well satisfied with the
tax system as it exists. The reformers complain that the growing erosion and corrosion of the income tax base should be corrected
promptly to permit continued reliance on this tax as the backbone of
the United States revenue system. Other critics argue that rates at
current levels have dangerously weakened incentives, and they in-
creasingly question how far we can extend our reliance on this form
of taxation.

Income Taxation and the Role of the Family

Any system of direct taxation that takes account of personal circumstances must provide for an appropriate unit of taxation. That
in personal taxation the unit must be related to the individual is
clear; but should it be the individual as such, or a married couple,
or a family, or a household? The concept of net income (later discussed) would be difficult enough to define even if it were not necessary to relate it to some spending unit. But individuals combine in
various ways that make it necessary to relate the concept to groups
as well as to "discreet similar units." In the case of these groups—
notably the family—expenditures are made for the good of the
whole and not primarily or exclusively for the benefit of the member

---

[4] Some comparative data are presented by Marion H. Bryden in "The Tax Mix in
Various Countries," *Canadian Tax Journal*, Vol. 10 (March–April, 1962) pp. 112–14.
They show the relative reliance on direct and indirect taxes in various countries. Direct
taxes as calculated include some levies other than income taxes, but property and land
taxes are classed as indirect. Comparison is made both for central governments and all
governments. As to the first, the United States leads the list with an impressive 85.5 percent of its total coming from direct levies; in the comparison of over-all systems the
United States is second to the Netherlands, 66.2 percent against 66.5 percent.

having legal title.[5] And power (influence) depending to a large extent on income is also family-oriented.[6] In this context, legal rights to income within the group are of superficial importance.

If groups of individuals are thus to be distinguished according to their responsibilities, or need, or power, what pattern of exemptions and/or rates will best provide equal treatment for equals (horizontal equity)? Are there special circumstances of age or prolonged dependency (as when taxpayers reach retirement or youths attend college) that should be recognized? Should the exemption system be supplemented by personal deductions that take account of some of these differences, particularly where the mother is employed and incurs expenses for the care of children? Are there considerations of revenue and incentive that support closing the gap between adjusted gross income and taxable income thus bringing statutory marginal and effective rates closer together even at the expense of equity? And so on.

The conference held to discuss these issues showed that there are profound differences of opinion on some of these matters.[7] The differences can be traced back to the ultimate criteria on which differentiation in taxation should be based, and they probably involve some differences in the concept of the family itself. Some critics support a division of family income by the number of individuals involved: "Each shall count for one and no more than one." Others contend that family groupings alter the taxpaying capacities of individuals and that considerations of welfare and/or power call for differential treatment. A few would make the answer turn on how benefits are allotted and decisions made within the family itself, and they suggest further research in this area.

The concept of the spending unit is central not only to personal income taxation but also to income distribution analysis. For example, it has been argued recently that comparisons of inequality in income distribution over time based on income tax statistics may be highly misleading if they take no account of changes in the unit of measurement that arise, not only from changes in the tax law, but

[5] William Vickrey, *Agenda for Progressive Taxation* (Ronald Press, 1947), p. 275.

[6] For a further discussion of the concept of "power" and its relation to taxation, see pp. 12, 95–96.

[7] See pp. 93–108.

also from changes in demography. Because the results are influenced by changes in statistics on marriage and divorce, wives in the labor force, and prolonged education, and by changes in various arrangements for the division of family wealth, they may not mean what they seem to imply.[8]

Exclusions and Rates

Frequently critics of the tax system say that the tax base must be broadened to reduce income tax rates. Unfortunately the statement suffers from ambiguities. Tax reform could involve: (1) a change in vertical distribution; (2) a change in horizontal distribution; or (3) a change in the relation of statutory rates to effective rates. The first could be accomplished by a disproportionate reduction in high-bracket rates or the enactment of a sales tax; the second, by closing certain alleged "loopholes," such as favors to capital gains, and reducing rates in each bracket enough to offset the increase in taxable income in that bracket; the third, by changes in income splitting, exemptions, and deductions. When it is said that the tax system must be reformed to improve economic incentive, any or all of these could be projected. The main point to be stressed here is that the base can be broadened within, as well as outside, the context of the income tax.

It is a well known fact that the income tax base accounts for less than half[9] of personal income as reckoned by the Department of Commerce. Some of this is a matter of conceptual differences and administrative leakage, but most of it is due to the personal exemptions and deductions presently allowed. These are largely adaptations of the law to suit family circumstances. Were they eliminated, a drastic reduction in rates without loss of revenue would be possible.

Categories of Rates

The graduated rate scale can be viewed in any one of three ways:

[8] Richard M. Titmuss, *Income Distribution and Social Change* (George Allen and Unwin, London, 1962).

[9] Our calculation for 1960 indicates that taxable income constitutes about 45 percent of total personal income.

first, there are the so-called *marginal* rates stated in the statute. Except in the case of taxable income that does not exceed the first bracket, they apply only to portions of income between the limits of successive brackets. Second, there are *average* rates, sometimes also called effective rates, on *taxable* income. As is usual in statistical series where incremental values trend upward, average rates lag behind marginal rates. If all brackets were of equal breadth, the average rate schedule would be simply the sum of the marginal rates divided by their number. Thus under the federal tax schedule, where the single taxpayer pays 20 percent on the first $2,000 of taxable income and 22 percent on the second $2,000, the average rate for a taxpayer with $4,000 of taxable income is 21 percent. Finally, there are *effective* rates, derived by dividing the taxpayer's total tax by his total income.

The marginal or incremental rate scale is accepted for the technical reason that it can provide a generally steady and consistent scale of progression covering even small increments of income. It avoids so-called notch problems: where rates are stated to cover entire incomes by classes of income, a taxpayer may find himself paying enough additional tax as he crosses a class line to have less disposable income than he would have had at a lower level of earnings.[10] Moreover, the difference between a rate scale stated in marginal terms and one stated in average terms may be regarded as a purely formal one. The same may not be true, however, of the third type of rate scale, which indicates the effective rate on all income, taxable and nontaxable. Effective rates differ radically from average rates because the latter are calculated without taking account of the exclusions in working from net income to the tax base. Moreover, two taxpayers with the same net income may pay radically different effective rates depending on the relative sums of the excluded items that apply in each case. To yield a given revenue, added exclusions would make higher marginal (and average) rates necessary, but effective rates may remain as before.

Whether high marginal rates as such, independent from the real

---

[10] Thus a taxpayer with $1,999 of net taxable income, were he to augment his income by $1 and thus subject his entire income to a higher rate, might find that he paid more in additional taxes than the increment to his income.

progression indicated by effective rates, have a deleterious effect on incentives will be considered in Chapter II.

Exclusions and Progression

A word should be added about the effect of exclusions on the progressivity of the tax system. Personal exemptions particularly are said to add to the progressivity of the system and indeed to constitute the principal source of progressivity within the first bracket of the federal tax schedule. Single taxpayers with net incomes of $2,000 or less pay at the same marginal and average rates, but their effective rates may range from zero to 15 percent depending on the size of their incomes within this income class.[11]

Exclusions from net income subject to a graduated tax are generally more valuable in terms of taxes saved to the rich than they are to the poor. On the other hand, the exclusion may constitute a smaller (or larger) proportion of income as incomes get larger. An exemption of a fixed sum per taxpayer, as in the case of the federal personal exemption, represents a decreasing proportion of income as income advances. This accounts for its contribution to progressivity.[12] But even if an exclusion is aimed at a progressive effect, it may be self-defeating if the revenue lost because of a reduced tax base is made good by a highly regressive substitute.

However, not all exclusions have a positive effect on income tax progression. Studies by Musgrave indicate that effective rates of tax, especially in the case of the higher income classes, are either not progressive at all or far less so than marginal or average rates.[13]

[11] Thus with the present statutory rate of 20 percent and an exemption of $600 the single taxpayer with income before exemption of $600 will pay at zero rate; at $1,200 he will pay at a 10 percent rate; at $1,800, at a 13.3 percent rate; and so on.

[12] Comparing rate scales for progressivity at different levels of yield is a highly technical exercise that may be avoided by the simple device of assuming that the government makes up the revenue lost as a result of the exclusion with a tax, such as a simple surtax, which is as progressive as the original. If the exclusion is proportional to income (and the tax scale is regularly progressive or regressive), the government can do this without distributional effects resulting from the exclusion. If the exclusion is more or less than proportional with rising income, the surtax will leave large taxpayers paying a lesser or larger share than formerly.

[13] Richard A. Musgrave, "How Progressive is the Income Tax?," in *Tax Revision Compendium* (cited in note 3), pp. 2223–34.

An exclusion proportional to income under proper assumptions[14] will have no distributional effects. This is but an application of the rule that a proportional subsidy to everybody is a subsidy to nobody. If the standard deduction in the federal law granted a percentage allowance to everybody without ceilings, its distributional effects would be nil. This would be true, however, only if the government made good its lost revenue with additions to rates as progressive as the original ones. It also assumes that all recipients of income pay a tax.

The Concept of Net Income

Most of the discussion of allowances for family differences starts with the assumption that there is a figure for net income and the question is how to tax it. But the concept of net income itself is not free of ambiguities. Of particular interest is the distinction between business expenses that are recognized as a negative item in calculating income and the personal or consumption expenses that are associated with the disposal of income. The distinction is not clear cut and may be especially troublesome at the boundary line. The maintenance of human beings who man the works can be regarded without too much distortion as a production cost like any other. In this view the cost of medical care is that of keeping one of the factors of production in repair much like the cost of maintaining a factory machine. The maintenance and education of children can be regarded as the cost of providing the requisite future labor force. A worker's expense of getting to and from the job is one that under modern conditions has to be paid in order to get goods produced. Expense-account entertainment both serves production and provides enjoyment for the host. If a banker maintains a farm more or less as a plaything, it is hard to characterize his losses from that farm as either a consumption expense or a business failure. And so on. Were we to attempt some guidelines for distinguishing consumption from production expense, we would probably conclude that: (1)

[14] The assumptions are that the income tax exclusion covers all income recipients and that the government will make up its lost revenue by taxes as progressive as the original (see note 12). Because of shifting from one bracket to another, the progression must also be regular.

consumption expenditures are not incurred mainly for the *purpose* of production; (2) they involve a larger element of choice; and (3) the division is a matter of degree.

Whatever may be said about marginal items, we may note that if the distinction between production and consumption expense were not made, very little indeed would be left for the income tax to tax. Were one to accept the idea that consumption outlays appropriate to one's station are a cost of maintaining the labor supply, one could easily stretch this doctrine to exclude all income from the tax base, except perhaps for savings, much of which in turn could be regarded as a necessary preparation for retirement. Thus, tenuous as the distinction between production cost and consumption may seem, it is the lifeline of the income tax.

Concept of Clear Income

No doubt in part because of the difficulty of distinguishing consumption from production expense, tax literature and tax practice have developed the concept of clear income. It consists of net income (adjusted gross income on the tax forms) minus an uncertain allowance to the taxpayer of personal expense money deemed sufficient to maintain himself and his dependents according to some biological or conventional standard. It is not among the concepts recognized by statisticians who compute various measures of national income in terms of relative achievement or economic performance. Not only is it argued that ability to pay begins only after these allowances have been covered; it is also contended that relative ability to pay must be reckoned only in terms of this least common denominator. The concept as we shall see plays a very important role in our inquiry—especially in the allowance of personal exemptions and deductions.

Ability to Pay and Progressive Taxation

The concept of ability to pay is often cited in tax disputes, but scholars (at least) have long recognized that it is a singularly ambiguous term. Probably everyone would agree that it calls for equal treatment of those whose relevant circumstances are the same. But this leaves for dispute the question of what circumstances are relevant and how far it is practical and expedient to recognize relevant differences. Many would argue that ability to pay also calls for some graduation in effective rates.

The classical justification of progression runs in terms of the diminishing utility of goods as more of them are acquired. Presumably a person's second automobile gives him less satisfaction than his first, and both are less important than a minimum outlay for food. Moreover, one person's outlay for a second automobile can be presumed to be less important to him than another's outlay for food is to the latter. One can move from this to compare their marginal incomes as such. If the decline in consumers' utility curves is faster than their rise in incomes, it follows that to take equally from taxpayers in terms of satisfaction, tax rates must be progressive. Moreover, any fall in the utility curve regardless of degree would justify progression if the aim is to minimize rather than to equalize sacrifice of satisfaction. However, the minimum sacrifice doctrine is strong medicine, and without qualification it leads to confiscation at the top of the income pyramid.[15]

This time-honored analysis has invited a barrage of persuasive criticism.[16] It involves interpersonal comparisons, thus ignoring the fact that A and B may have different capacities to enjoy the good things that income makes available. The hedonistic calculus is introspective; subjective reactions are not susceptible to measurement, at least not with the degree of precision that tax legislation requires. People would probably not be satisfied to distribute taxes according to aversion to them even if they could. Declining utility is a theory of consumption, and the legitimacy of extending it to the satisfactions derived from owning stocks and bonds is questionable. And so on.

Persuasive rejoinders have been offered to some of these objections. It is said that individual variations from the average capacity for enjoyment will be random and can be ignored in dealing with large numbers of people, as taxation must. While measurement and comparison of subjective reactions can never be precise, it can give us adequate approximations.

A largely alternative approach to progressive taxation seeks to weigh the issue in terms of its social, political, and economic

---

[15] Each dollar taken from a richer taxpayer is presumed to involve less sacrifice than one taken from a poorer taxpayer until the two are reduced to the same income level.

[16] See for instance Walter J. Blum and Harry Kalven, Jr., *The Uneasy Case for Progressive Taxation* (University of Chicago Press, 1953).

effects.[17] Equity of policies here is rated according to their service or disservice to social objectives. It is conceded that this, like all other approaches to progressive taxation, yields no answers concerning which reasonable men may not differ. But it is said at least to lead to a more realistic analysis.

Of special interest to us here are the distinct considerations of minimum amenities and of power which this approach invites. Welfare is viewed socially as a matter of conserving human resources that are important for production, national defense, and the success of democratic decision-making. Power is a complex concept that not only includes the economic elements of equal opportunity for youth and dispersion of control in production and consumption decisions; it involves also the control over the means of communication which can exert vast influence over the prevailing image of social and political values. Minorities accept a majority decision with grace if they are really free (and have some power) to persuade others and make converts; they conspire against the system when they are impotent to do this. Considerations of power are at the root of such judgments as the one that says a substantial middle class is a prerequisite for the success and stability of democracy. The concern about power is no doubt an important element in the larger concern about distribution and inequalities; it thus in some sense applies to the entire scale though it is overshadowed by welfare considerations in the lower ranges of income.

The above approach to progressive taxation and particularly its division into considerations of minimum amenities and power is, as we shall see, highly relevant to the problem of income splitting, which will be treated in Chapter IV. Proponents argue that progression at the bottom of the scale is a matter of conserving human resources, and as such it looks to the number of people in the family whose amenities it seeks to maintain. Progression at the top of the scale is justified as a means of checking and dispersing power. The latter is a family affair, and comparisons must be made in terms of the aggregates of income or wealth received or owned and controlled by family members.

[17] See Elmer D. Fagen, "Recent and Contemporary Theories of Progressive Taxation," *Journal of Political Economy*, Vol. 46 (August 1938), pp. 457–97; Harold M. Groves, "Toward a Social Theory of Progressive Taxation," *National Tax Journal*, Vol. 9 (March 1956), pp. 27–34.

Judgments about exemptions for dependents also depend on an underlying philosophy of progressive taxation. On the classical approach, one is all but constrained to agree with Pigou[18] that exemption allowances are pertinent at all levels of income and should moreover increase with income. This leads logically to the conclusion that exemptions should take the form of a percentage of income rather than a flat per capita sum. If A and B are two millionaires and A has a family of four and B one of three, adequate differentiation would appear to require more than an additional $600 exclusion for A. Millionaires can be expected to maintain the junior members of their families according to the standards of the parents.

The alternative approach, on the other hand, would favor a system that allowed exemptions as a decreasing function of income. Going beyond the present system, which does this to some extent, proponents of this dispensation would probably recommend confining exemptions to the lower (or lowest) classes (class) of income recipients. The number of members in a family is relevant to a minimum-amenities but not to a power philosophy. Beyond the lower brackets of income, a family's choice of another child is its free choice in the disposition of its income but not a concern of the public's. Having cared for its interest in the health and education of children either through direct government outlays or through the allowance of a tax-free minimum, the public turns to the progressive income tax to moderate excessive concentration of power. In this view, if the family's choice is of concern to the state at all, an addition to its ranks might call for increasing rather than decreasing its tax because such addition will augment the demand for public services.

The Austerity School

What may be termed the austerity school of income tax proponents[19] prefers this tax because it affords the widest opportunity for taxation with minimal effects on the private allocation of resources. Some unneutral effects are inevitable; in some sense the pro-

---

[18] A. C. Pigou, *A Study in Public Finance* (Macmillan, London, 1928), pp. 101–03.

[19] See Henry Simons, *Personal Income Taxation* (University of Chicago Press, 1938): *Federal Tax Reform* (University of Chicago Press, 1950).

gressive scale is one, and it is acceptable as a means of reducing inequalities. All exceptions and exclusions must carry a high burden
of proof; in case of doubt the decision should favor revenue needs.
This position is further supported on the ground that politicians do
better when they adhere to general rules; if they start making exceptions, there is no end to the process, and the outcome is dictated
more by group pressures than by a high regard for the public interest. Those who take this position are forever at war with what they
call "loopholes." The term is not a precise one, but it can be
stretched to include many of the exemptions and deductions we will
consider here. They look askance at the high-rate, low-base pattern
that the federal income tax has developed. Rather than move to
what they consider inferior taxes, they would recommend a return
to the principles of uniformity, universality, and consistency, from
which they feel that the present practice and trend have departed.

Summary and Conclusions

The problems that this book considers are normative ones on
which no factual research can lead to definitive answers. They are
none the less critical and in need of analytical attention on that
account. A fresh study of this subject might delineate the fundamental criteria on which rational decisions must be made. Beyond
this, there are the facts of history, of comparative practices, and of
legal constraints that should illuminate the issues. Illustrative calculations of revenue effects and of comparative burdens under various
alternative proposals might serve a catalytical role in the analysis.
Some empirical data, particularly those developed in budget studies, are relevant, and, as indicated by the conference discussion,
there may be some gaps here that should be highlighted.

The tax criterion that makes the most sense, at least at the bottom of the income scale, is that of comparative welfare viewed either
as a matter of relative sacrifice (in meeting tax bills) or as one of
preserving and conserving the private amenities in which there is an
obvious social interest. In applying this standard to families of various sizes, the question is raised: What combination of income and
family size can "live as well" as some other combination? Unfortunately, the standard is difficult to apply in the middle and upper
ranges of income. Moreover, it is in these ranges that the public

concern about power may overshadow that about amenities. As was observed above, the welfare philosophy lends some support for splitting and for exemptions that are maintained or increased with rising incomes. The power approach, on the other hand, lends no support for splitting and points toward exemptions that are a decreasing function of income (vanishing exemption or tax credit).

Personal Exemptions

With regard to personal exemption practices, it is difficult to discern any verdict of history in either American experience or that of other countries, several of which have added direct family allowances to a variety of other institutions. Exemptions for taxpayer and spouse and dependents serve the three functions of excluding some taxpayers from any tax; of providing or adding to graduation; and of differentiation. The second function could, with some difficulty, be carried out in large part without distributional effects by direct manipulation of rates instead.

The absolute size of exemptions may differ from that indicated by personal budget studies in the interests both of wide participation in direct taxpaying and of revenue; relative exemptions have far less reason for such departure (which at present is considerable). Failure to allow the exclusion of at least the minimum amount recognized for welfare budgets costs dearly in terms of human resources; more protection here could be financed if exemptions were confined to their original (British) purpose of excluding the poorest residents. A tax credit would serve the same end less logically but more simply.

As to techniques, five types of exemption procedure are distinguished: initial exemptions, vanishing exemptions, continuing exemptions, tax credits, and percentage-of-income allowances. (These types are explained in detail on pages 34–38.) The present continuing exemption can be supported on the assumption that size of family requires differentiation at all income levels. However, even more differentiation could be achieved by using percentage-of-income allowances, and this device might also serve as a flexible substitute for splitting or partial splitting. The case for a vanishing exemption, or the simpler and less drastic tax credit, rests on the assumption that consideration neither of equity nor of other social goals requires much, if any, differentiation except at the bottom of the scale.

Conservative policy with regard to exemptions allows, without loss of revenue, for moderated marginal rates which may or may not conserve incentives. In considering the effects of taxes on incentives it is necessary to distinguish differences between (a) nominal marginal rates due to deductions and exemptions and (b) true marginal and effective rates due to the degree of progressivity. The latter is probably more significant, but there are grounds for the view that the nominal rate structure, quite aside from distributional effects, is also of no small importance.

The special (sometimes double) exemption provided in the parent-student situation is criticized on the score that it is ill-designed to promote education and unfortunate in its vertical incidence. Reform proposals recommend either confining such exemption to earned income or earned income plus a special allowance for earned income that would be available to the student only or to the parent also if he reported such income along with his own. Conference discussion suggested that the problem be reconsidered along with exemption for minors (with income) generally.

Personal deductions aim largely at differentiation, and since the standard deduction has abandoned this objective, it may as well be built into the rate scale along with a provision that only deductions that exceed a specified percentage of income will be allowed.

The Aged

The considerable array of institutions designed to ease the income tax for the aged are all highly vulnerable to objection. The exemption of Old Age and Survivors' Insurance benefits was an historical accident, this one illustrating the hazards of augmenting subsidies with tax concessions. If the retirement credit was ever worth the complications it brought to income tax accounting, the day passed with wider coverage by social security. The double exemption is not supported by budgetary studies of cost of living at different ages, and it gives a bonanza to the considerable number of wealthy old people. The special medical care provisions are ineffective for those who need them most. And so on. The whole development lends support to spokesmen for the austerity school, who contend that a net income tax should tax net income and should differentiate beyond this only through a conservative exemption and graduated rates.

Income Splitting

Income splitting in the United States is the product of historical developments rather than design, and there is reason to believe that its bizarre changes in pre-existing tax distribution were never carefully weighed or intended. Proper relative burden on single taxpayers and couples is not scientifically determinable, but a persuasive case can be made for the view that the present practice unduly burdens single people and favors particularly the one-job family that "has married into lower brackets." Various promising alternatives, all of them involving variations of a dual-rate schedule, are discussed in this study. However, the conference discussion revealed a considerable following for the view that splitting only recognizes that each shall count for one and no more than one. Alternative approaches are regarded by this school of thought as objectionable on the score that they view spouses and children as articles of consumption.

The attempted relief of single persons through special provision for householders and widows and widowers is weak in rationale and has little to commend it otherwise.

Differentiation between married couples with two jobs and those with one is at least as compelling as that between married couples and single persons. Such differentiation might be effected by dual-rate scales, a special exemption, or a deduction for special expenses (preferably in proportion to the wife's earnings and with a ceiling), such as that now allowed (somewhat niggardly) for child care. More generous allowance for child care might also be considered.

The subject of our study, as was pointed out earlier in this introductory chapter, invites considerable re-examination as to detail; the detail should be conceived against an underlying philosophy that will stand the test of rationality.

CHAPTER II

Exemptions

TAX DIFFERENTIATION AMONG families can be accomplished in a variety of ways. One of these is splitting (discussed in Chapter IV), which is not effective at the lower levels of income. Personal exemption is another device, and it is effective principally at the lower levels of income. However, exemptions serve a variety of purposes, of which differentiation is only one. Following Seltzer[1] we observe that the personal exemptions perform at least three functions:

1. They exclude from the tax base entirely the earnings of the lowest strata of income recipients.

2. They provide a factor of graduation, especially important for the income class associated with the first bracket in the scale; here all the graduation is supplied by the personal exemption.

3. They differentiate among families according to the number of dependents and provide a special concession to the aged and the blind.

Some preliminary comments may be made about this list of functions. It is noted that the first does not require an exemption for everybody; it requires only an exclusion of income recipients from tax if their incomes fall below a minimum.

[1] Lawrence H. Seltzer, "The Place of the Personal Exemptions in the Present-Day Income Tax," testimony submitted to the House Committee on Ways and Means, *Tax Revision Compendium*, Vol. 1 (November 1959), pp. 508–09.

The second factor particularly raises interesting questions about the relation between exemptions and graduated rates. To what degree can exemptions and graduation be substituted for each other? And if they can play the same role, which is preferable? These questions will be discussed in a later section of this chapter.

Differentiation involves the matter of criteria discussed in the introductory chapter. More specifically it involves a question of degree and whether it should be confined to lower brackets or maintained through a constant, increasing, or decreasing allowance. Differentiation could also be achieved by graduation, but this would require a separate rate scale for each family size.

United States and Foreign Experience

As will be seen in Table 1, both the level and the pattern of family exemptions in the United States have undergone many changes since 1913. The original federal law allowed a single person a $3,000 exemption, a married couple, $4,000, and no additional allowance for dependents. Starting with a system that allowed a married couple one and one-third times as much as a single person, the ratio was later changed to $2\frac{1}{2}$ times as much (1932–40). Allowances for children have generally increased both absolutely and relatively. The equal per-capita arrangement was inaugurated in 1944 as a part of an income-tax simplification program, and it has endured to the present. In 1948 per-capita exemptions were raised from $500 to $600, where they now stand.

Between 1929 and the middle 1950's, says Seltzer,[2] "the Federal individual income tax was transformed from one that applied to only 4 percent of the population, including taxpayers and their dependents, and to only 30 percent of individual incomes, to one that covered about 70 percent of the population and more than four-fifths of the greatly enlarged total of individual incomes." Major factors in the transformation were a drastic reduction in personal exemptions (excepting only those for dependents) and the rise in personal incomes, in part due to inflation and in part to economic growth. The importance of the reduction in personal

[2] *Ibid.*, p. 493.

TABLE 1. Major Changes in Federal Personal Exemptions Since 1913

Year	Single Persons	Married persons		Children	
		Amount	As percent of single persons' exemption	Amount	As percent of single persons' exemption
1913	$3,000	$4,000	133	$ 0	0
1917	1,000	2,000	200	200	20
1921	1,000	2,500	250	400	40
1925	1,500	3,500	233	400	27
1932	1,000	2,500	250	400	40
1940	800	2,000	250	400	50
1941	750	1,500	200	400	53
1942	500	1,200	240	350	70
1944	500	1,000	200	500	100
1948	600	1,200	200	600	100

exemptions in this change is indicated by Seltzer's calculation that, were the 1929 schedule applied under conditions prevailing in 1955, the Treasury would have lost about 45 percent of its revenue from this tax. The reduction also was responsible in considerable part for an impressive shift in tax liability among income groups. Under the old income tax taxpayers with net incomes of $25,000 or more accounted for nearly 93 percent of all revenue; those with incomes below $10,000 for a little more than 1 percent; the corresponding figures in 1955 were 22 percent and 61 percent.[3] It is clear enough that in the interlude between 1929 and the middle 1950's the income tax evolved from a class to a mass tax.

Not to be slighted either are the roles of inflation and economic growth in the transformation. The consumer price index rose from 102.8 to 125.7 between 1948 and 1960, and this rise in effect cut personal exemptions about one-fifth, thus canceling out the increase in exemptions in 1948 from $500 to $600. One of the unwanted and sometimes unrealized effects of inflation is to change the pattern of the income tax considerably without benefit of Congressional action.

The experience of the states has been similar in some respects but less pronounced, with state exemptions generally higher than

[3] *Ibid.*, pp. 500–01.

federal, and the per capita system, though copied on a considerable scale, as yet followed by only a minority of states. Thorson[4] calculated the median exemption for single persons, married couples, and dependents at $1,000, $2,000, and $300 respectively as of 1940; and $1,000, $2,500, and $600 as of 1961. An innovation, starting in Wisconsin in 1927, substituted a tax credit for the income allowance; it has since been adopted by six states. The implications of this institution will be discussed later. Here it may be further observed that the states with high exemptions frequently have adopted a retail sales tax to supplement their income tax or vice versa. In some cases the two taxes are regarded as a balanced program to attain a desired incidence of distribution. Put another way, the sales tax is regarded as the easy way to collect considerable revenue from the lower strata of income recipients and the income tax as the means of insuring that the rich pay "their share."

Municipal income taxes in the United States typically have allowed no personal exemptions at all. Largely collected at the source and applied to a broad base with low rates, they have been surprisingly productive. This experience is a reminder of the fact frequently overlooked that an income tax is a highly flexible device and can be applied without the refinements we have come generally to associate with it. Or, to put it another way, there are alternatives within the income tax field which make it unnecessary, whether or not desirable, to look outside this institution for more revenue. Some critics argue that the income tax has proved so amenable to differentiation, and differentiations cost so much in terms of the tax base, that it has been necessary to apply excessive rates to the residue in order to get the required revenue.

There has been a wide variety of foreign experience[5] with personal exemptions. In Australia and India a single person is entitled to an exemption only if his income does not exceed a certain amount. This could be based on the idea that since everybody qualifies potentially as a single taxpayer (or one of his dependents) and everything is relative in taxation, it is unnecessary to include single

[4] Douglas Y. Thorson, "The Selection of a Tax Unit Under the Income Tax," (Ph.D. thesis, University of Wisconsin, 1962), p. 169*n*.

[5] Reliance here is mostly on Thorson, *ibid.*, pp. 175–79; John F. Due, "The Fiscal Structure of European Countries," reprinted from *Collectanea de Estudos* (No. 12, 1961), Centro de Estudos de Estatística Económica, Lisboa, Portugal.

individuals in a differentiation system. Historically the British until 1909 confined the personal exemption to taxpayers with incomes below a specified minimum and without distinction between single persons and those with spouse and dependents. The present British system is unusually elaborate: the personal exemption applies to the standard tax and not the surtax. For the standard tax, both an earned income concession and a special earned income allowance for working wives are provided. South Africa uses a tax credit system.

Several countries vary the exemption for dependent children according to the order and number of the children. In some of these, the exemption increases more than proportionately with children beyond the first, but in Australia and West Germany the reverse is true. In West Germany the amount allowed is less with each successive child.[6] This procedure, as we shall see, finds some support in budget studies, and it could be based on the view that population growth (or at any rate, large families) should not be encouraged by the income tax. Several countries rely heavily for differentiation on multiple rate schedules. This is true in Denmark and Sweden, which provide such schedules for married couples and single persons and make no further differentiation. Finland uses three schedules and the Netherlands an independent schedule for each family size.

In addition, several countries supplement personal exemptions by distributing family allowances. This practice applies a positive approach to sharing the cost of child care and extends assistance to those whose income is so low that the dependents' exemption is unavailable.[7]

It is apparent from the above review that there is no "natural

---

[6] But see note 7.

[7] These allowances may or may not be correlated with the system of income tax exemptions. The Canadian program in 1957 started with a positive subsidy for children amounting to $5 a month for babies and more for older children. The dependents' income tax allowance was reduced from $400 to $150 in the case of subsidized children. ("Mr. Woolley and the Income Tax," *Canadian Tax Journal*, Vol. 5 [January–February 1957], pp. 20–22; Joseph W. Willard, "Family Allowances in Canada," *International Labour Review*, Vol. 75 [March 1957], pp. 207–29). In Sweden, with the inauguration of family allowances, personal exemptions for dependents were dropped entirely. (Anna-Lisa Kälvesten, "Family Policy in Sweden," *Marriage and Family Living*, Vol. 17 [August 1955], pp. 250–54). There are no allowances after two children in India, but allowances increase after the first child in Finland, France, Israel, and Germany.

order" about an exemption system. Different views about what is equitable or other considerations seem to have prevailed in various countries, and the random variations of historical circumstances no doubt played a considerable role.

Rationale of Exemptions

We have already suggested much that is relevant to the topics in this section, and here we may confine ourselves to their philosophical aspects.

Equity

In terms of equity, exemptions are defended mainly on the ground that a rigorous application of the ability-to-pay doctrine requires that taxes be based on clear income rather than total income. Several forms of this argument may be distinguished. The first and simplest, but perhaps not the most persuasive, is that the taxpayer's expenses of maintenance are in some sense a production outlay analogous to a businessman's expense of doing business and/or maintaining his capital. This approach was considered in Chapter I, where it was noted that the line between production and consumption is tenuous and especially difficult at their common border, but that, were the line to be obliterated, a respectable base for the income tax could hardly be maintained.[8] Moreover, if personal maintenance were deductible, it might seem appropriate to allow it in proportion to income. This would bring it under the rule that proportional subtractions have few if any distributional consequences and serve mainly to raise marginal rates.

Taking another approach, one can support a minimum allowance for subsistence on the ground that it involves the alternatives of life or death, and the importance of these fundamentals to the individual is not commensurate with that of other goods. In terms of incidence, it was argued by the classical economists that taxes on minimum subsistence are ineffective in any case: they reduce the supply of labor and result in an increase in wages to recoup the tax.

---

[8] This is not to argue that there are no personal expenses directly related to a job that should be allowed as income tax deductions.

This line of thought has not been accepted by all critics. Some have argued that government (at least minimum government) is a necessity like any other and that its cost accordingly should be included in the minimum family budget along with other costs. To this, however, it might be rejoined that since the affluent society (at least) proposes to maintain a minimum for everybody by welfare programs of government, this austere approach only introduces the waste of circularity.

Clear income can be defended, not only as the basis for measuring minimum allowances, but also as the medium to which total income must be reduced to make significant comparisons among taxpayers at all levels. It is as important, it can be argued, to distinguish between one-hundred-thousand-dollar incomes in terms of family responsibilities as it is to do so for thousand-dollar incomes.

As was noted in the introduction to this study, the alternative socio-economic philosophy of tax distribution views the problem largely in terms of the maintenance of human resources at the bottom of the scale and of the concentration of power at the top. As we have said, this approach supports the view that exemptions are important only at the bottom of the scale, where consideration of human resources calls for differentiation on the basis of the number of people involved. As to the upper end of the scale, where power is important, this latter is a matter of families, and the numbers involved in each are of no social concern. In this view, the decision of a millionaire to enlarge his family rather than choose some other extension of his consumption or his investments is his own to make and should have no bearing on his taxes. [9]

Almost everyone concedes that considerations of equity must be tempered with other interests, of which a few of the more important are discussed here.

Revenue

Exemptions are extremely important for the federal revenue, and this consideration, probably more than any other, has dictated the choice of exemption levels and patterns. For instance, "during World War II, when there was an overriding need for revenue,

---

[9] It may be noted that this line of argument disregards eugenics; perhaps it assumes that tax distribution has no effect on differential birth rates.

Congress reduced the exemptions drastically, without nice calculations of tolerable living standards."[10] Seltzer compares the revenue
cost of a $200 increase in personal exemptions with an alternative
rate reduction from the present 20 percent to 10 percent on the first
$1,000 of taxable income. Based on 1955 data, the former would
cost $5 billion and the latter, $6 billion.[11] Rough calculations of the
revenue effects of various tax reduction measures in 1962 indicate
the following: raising the per capita exemptions from $600 to $700
would cost $3 billion; a reduction of 10 percent in everybody's final
tax would cost $4.8 billion; reducing all tax rates by 5 percentage
points would cost $10.2 billion; reducing only the first bracket rate
by 5 percentage points would cost $6.4 billion. The distributive
effects of these alternatives are obviously quite different. Reducing
the first bracket rate or raising the exemption concentrates the tax
relief to some degree in the lower brackets. But it does not confine
such relief to the poorer taxpayers.

If no over-all revenue reduction is contemplated, an increase in
exemptions may require the development of alternative sources outside the income tax. Principal candidates would probably be a
general sales tax or one or more specific excises. Defending a modest
exemption level, critics then argue that the distributional effects
and other consequences of the alternative source would be more
undesirable than austere allowances under the net income tax.

They also argue that taxing small incomes may be warranted as
compared with the alternative of reduced government spending, on
the ground that the benefit the poor may receive from augmented
public services is more than commensurate with the prospective
sacrifices.

Participation

Governments necessarily spend a great deal of "other peoples'
money." It is argued that the process is likely to work better, and the
morale of the taxpayer to be more readily sustained, if a large part
of the voting public pays direct taxes. The feeling is that those who
direct the government should have a share in the consequences.

Our present system of exemptions, when added to the other pro-

[10] Seltzer, *op. cit.*, p. 512.
[11] *Ibid.*

visions of the existing law, excludes about 30 percent of the population from tax-paying units. Exemptions themselves on nontaxable returns total $23,977 million, which is about 7.6 percent of the total reported adjusted gross income.[12]

High exclusions from an income tax lead to a regressive tax system for taxpayers at the bottom of the scale and for those entirely excluded. Thus, if all income below $5,000 were excluded, the incidence of taxes on incomes below this amount would be dictated solely by consumption and other regressive taxes, and the taxpayer with a $5,000 net income might contribute at a lesser rate than one with a $4,000 net income.

Administration

No doubt a defense for some exclusions can be made on the score that they reduce the number of returns requiring attention from tax administrators. The strength and validity of this consideration has been generally weakened by the development of the techniques and practice of withholding. Moreover, wherever one draws the line as to participation there must always be some taxpayers slightly above it whose tax is so small as to have been hardly worth the attention of the revenue authorities.

Size of Exemptions

The questions to which we address ourselves in this section are: (1) What level of personal exemptions is adequate? (2) How should they be distributed among family groups of varying sizes?

One hypothesis is that the exemptions (at least at the bottom of the scale) should approximate a maintenance standard of living. Using this approach to the problem, one would hope for guidance from budget studies. However, as the authors of such studies are the first to insist, the standards of adequacy used are subjective standards. Samuelson[13] summarizes the adequacy of budgets (for an average family of four in 1960) as follows: bare subsistence, $2,500; minimum health and decency, $3,650; and minimum comfort, $4,450.

[12] Seltzer has a further discussion of population and income not taxed because of exemptions. *Op. cit.*, p. 493.

[13] Paul A. Samuelson, *Economics* (5th ed.; McGraw-Hill, 1961), pp. 113–14.

The following definitions are given: (1) Bare subsistence—no movies, practically no meat, no dental care, no newpapers, little clothing, and so forth. (2) Minimum health and decency—occasional movie or recreational expenditure, cheap cuts of meat at intervals, some medical and dental care, and so forth. (3) Minimum comfort—adequate diet, occasional vacation and amusement, some tobacco and books, and so forth. It will be observed that the $2,667 exclusion allowed under our income tax law (including the standard deduction), while slightly greater than the bare subsistence figure above, hardly represents what Americans would say that most Americans should have. The numbers which even our present exemptions exclude are also an indication of the extent of poverty in the "affluent society."

No doubt the bare subsistence budget described above is not the "rock bottom" minimum necessary to survive biologically under prescribed conditions. Life goes on in various parts of the world and also in the United States on much less. But there are psychological elements involved, and it would be dangerous to conclude that production and the working force under American conditions could be maintained if many people were to enjoy much less for long.

However, it can be argued that there is no conclusive case for the proposition that exemptions must follow budget studies in terms of absolute levels. Considerations of equity and welfare must be weighed against those of participation and revenue, and a compromise below budget indications may be warranted. But it should be noted that impingement on minimum standards at *some* selected level comes at a high price in terms of personal and social objectives. Question may also be raised whether it makes sense to provide minimum exclusions that are less than welfare budgets.[14]

We must note again that an exemption as an exclusion of taxpayers from the income tax and an exemption which is extended to everybody are two quite different phenomena. The first is necessary to preserve minimum amenities; the second is only a convenient

[14] Some study of welfare budgets involving categorical state and federal aids in Wisconsin indicates that in the case of a family of four or more, present income tax allowances are adequate to cover welfare allowances, but that in the case of smaller families, especially where adults only (and below age 65) are involved, they fall considerably short. In these welfare budgets much depends on variable factors such as shelter cost and medical expense, and in the case of larger families, the age of the children.

way of graduating rates and providing differentials. The tax cost of a continuing exemption as compared with that of a minimum exclusion, and how much the elimination of the former would extend the latter if applied to that end, has not been estimated precisely. But there can be no doubt that both figures are substantial even if allowance is made for accommodating the notch problem. Moreover, the idea is infinitely flexible. An exemption of $500 per capita vanishing at the rate of 25 cents per dollar of income increment, combined with dividing the present first bracket into quarters with rates of 5, 10, 15, and 20 percent on each successive $500 of income, would lower the tax burden for most low-income taxpayers, conserve revenue, and place more reliance on the graduated scale than does our present system. It can be argued that the inclusion of some welfare clients as taxpayers is less important than relieving the very tough bite of the initial tax rate. The principal objection to splitting the first bracket is that it would aggravate difficulties in withholding. For taxpayers with wages as their only source of income and with incomes up to $4,000 if married, the present system provides an easy approximation of taxes due with a single rate of withholding.

Whatever may be said about budget studies as a guide for the *absolute* levels of exemptions, a much stronger case can be made for them as the basis of *relative* exemptions. And in this latter respect again the departures appear to be many and wide in the present federal income tax. However, as we shall see, a rational defense can be made for some of them.

What do the budget studies show with regard to relative cost of living by families of different size? They indicate first of all that it costs a married couple less than twice what it does to maintain a single person at the same standard of living—probably about 1.4 times as much.

It may also be noted that the per capita system as applied to married couples is on the generous side and that this is an addition to the substantial benefits of splitting. It would indeed appear that nobody loves a bachelor!

Budget studies also indicate that the cost of maintaining children is substantially less than that of maintaining adults and that the cost decreases as more children are added to the family.[15]

[15] Reed Hansen gives the results of ten such studies as follows: "To summarize, ten rather extensive budget studies can be utilized to determine whether family unit

A rational defense can be made for the per capita system insofar as it gives more generous allowances for dependent children than for adults. The allowance for the taxpayer, and to a lesser extent for his spouse, fills a different function than that for dependents. The allowance for the taxpayer to some extent, even though imperfectly, comes under the rule that a concession to everybody is a concession to nobody. At least it is in the area where the substitution of rate manipulation for exemptions is most feasible. In other words, the need for differentiation begins with the dependents. No one claims that the $600 allowance for dependents is higher than the actual necessary cost of maintaining them under most circumstances at least at any scale beyond the barest minimum.

The failure to take any account of economies of scale that attend families with more than one child can be defended, if at all, only on the ground of simplicity, which indeed is the historical reason for the per capita system.

Differentials Ignored

It should be noted that the exemptions at best are rough approximations of living costs and make no allowance for such material factors as differences in cost due to geographical location, special vocational needs, taxpayer's position in the life cycle (except the double exemption of the elderly), and, above all, year-to-year fluctuations in income. The latter lead into the large problem of averaging income over time. It is recognized that the stake of the small income taxpayer in a system of averaging that would treat unused personal exemptions as a loss is very high. Either a carry-over or a carry-back, or both, would be valuable in different circumstances, the former in the case of a student for instance, the latter in the case of one about to retire and live off his savings. Levy notes

---

costs change with changing family size. In all ten studies, budgetary evidence supports the contention that large families enjoy economies of scale and experience decreasing unit costs. . . ."

On the basis of four budget studies, he selects the following average relative cost pattern, starting with single persons and proceeding to add spouse and children: 70: 100: 128: 153: 174: 195. He suggests that a 2–4–1–½ ratio most closely fits the pattern of relative costs but would be willing to settle for a 2–4–1 pattern as representing a fair approximation (married couple twice single taxpayer and dependents half as much as single taxpayer). (Reed Robert Hansen, "The Tax Treatment of Family Income," [Ph.D. thesis, University of Wisconsin, 1959], pp. 126, 131, 139.)

that "a carry-back would increase the countercyclical properties of the income tax while avoiding the awkward question of the starting point of the averaging period, which would have to be determined in the case of a carry-forward."[16] The statement calls attention to one of the difficulties in all averaging devices, which is that they fail to take account of the imputed value of leisure. One who enjoys a sabbatical year even without pay is surely favored by averaging that counts the income of that year as zero.

As will be noted later, the personal deductions may also be regarded as supplementary differentiated exemptions. Deductions, exemptions, graduation, and splitting are at least first cousins and to some degree substitutes for each other.

Exemption Mechanics and Economic Effects

As for substitution, it is not very difficult to express a continuing exemption[17] in terms of net income instead of taxable income.[18] This can be done by simply assigning a zero rate to the exempted portion and applying rates to net income as they are currently applied to taxable income, with all bracket limits raised by the amount of the exemption. Thus the present scale for a single person would read as follows: First $600 of net income, 0 percent; net income above $600 and not exceeding $2,600, 20 percent; and so on. The conversion would of course require a separate schedule for each family size. Dr. Levy has also demonstrated that "any progressive tax with a lineally declining exemption can be expressed as a progressive tax with a continuing exemption." His example of this[19] shows what one would

---

[16] Michael E. Levy, *Income Tax Exemptions* (North Holland Publishing Company, Amsterdam, 1960).

[17] The term is taken from Michael Levy's work where he distinguishes four types of exemption procedure: *initial* exemption, which provides an exclusion of minimum income for those whose incomes do not exceed this amount; *vanishing* exemption, like the initial exemption except that the exclusion is so managed that it disappears gradually with mounting income; *continuing* exemption, which is a constant amount at all income levels; and *tax credits*, by which a constant value in taxes saved is allowed at all levels. (Levy, *op. cit.*)

[18] The term "net income" is here used to mean simply present taxable income plus personal exemptions.

[19] The example is as follows: He assumes a $500 exemption and a declining factor of 25 cents on a dollar of income so that the exemption will disappear completely at

expect—namely, that under the vanishing exemption the needed statutory marginal rates are substantially lower.[20]

Is it possible within the framework of constant revenue and constant relative burden to reduce marginal rates for everybody by eliminating a general exclusion? The answer must take account first of the fact that there are two sets of marginal rates involved, one that attends the effective rates (on net income) and one that attends the statutory rates (on taxable income).[21]

Since our question assumes no change in revenue or distribution, effective rates and the marginal rates that attend them are presumed

---

$2,500. "At a net income level of $2,000, for example, the total tax liability is $375, computed either as a (lineally declining) exemption of $125, plus $62.50 (.10×625) on the first $625 of taxable income, plus $125 (.20×625) on the next $625 of taxable income, plus $187.50 (.30×625) on the third $625 of taxable income; or alternately as a (continuing) exemption of $500, plus $62.50 (.125×500) on the first $500 of taxable income, plus $125 (.250×500) on the next $500 of taxable income, plus $187.50 (.375×500) on the third $500 of taxable income." (*Op. cit.*, p. 23.)

[20] The declining exemption also avoids the so-called "notch problem," which embarrasses an initial exemption with its abrupt termination. For example, if incomes up to $600 were not taxed at all and incomes over $600 were taxed in full, almost any practical statutory marginal rate would be confiscatory at the margin above the exemption.

[21] A simple model will illustrate this. Suppose we wish to collect from incomes of $2,000, $3,000, and $4,000 at effective rates of 2, 3, and 4 percent respectively. The taxes paid in this case would be $40, $90, and $160 respectively. Incremental rates on respective $1,000 additions to the $2,000 income would be 5 percent and 7 percent. Now suppose that half of all income were exempt. Effective rates could be preserved by taxing $1,000 of *taxable* income at 4 percent; $1,500, at 6 percent; and $2,000, at 8 percent. Or, in terms of incremental rates, the first $500 increment to a $1,000 base must pay at 10 percent and the second at 14 percent. Now suppose the exemption takes the form of a lump sum of $1,000 for each taxpayer. To get the $40, $90, and $160 from the respective taxpayers, effective rates on *taxable* income must be 4 percent, $4\frac{1}{2}$ percent, and $5\frac{1}{3}$ percent on taxable income classes. Each $1,000 of income above the first would carry an incremental rate of 5 percent and 7 percent respectively.

Three observations are noted: (1) The exclusion necessitates higher statutory marginal rates on taxable income in each case because the "jumps" from the initial rates occur at lower levels than they would were the exclusion disallowed. (2) The effective incremental rate (marginal rate) is the same regardless of the method of achieving progression; in all cases a taxpayer with a $2,000 income has to pay $50 extra if he increases his income by $1,000 and $70 extra if he increases it by $2,000; this is implicit in the progressive scale of rates. (3) The width of the brackets remains constant in the case of the lump-sum exclusion because the latter's effect is exhausted in the effective rate on the first bracket of income.

to remain constant.[22] But this is not true of statutory marginal rates, which can be reduced by narrowing the gap between taxable income and net income. To take the simplest possible example, suppose that everybody were allowed half of each dollar of net (adjusted gross) income, including prospective increments and decrements, as an exemption. Removing such an exemption would permit the halving of all statutory rates and the doubling of all statutory brackets.

Would this have any advantage? It can be argued persuasively that it would not. In terms of incentives a person with a $10,000 income contemplating a decision to add or not to add $1,000 to this net income would pay the same tax on both his present income and the increment no matter how the statute brought about the effective rate and its progression.

However, several qualifications to this answer warrant attention. Even though it be conceded that under the rigorous assumptions imposed by our question, the means of the levy makes only a formal difference, the latter may be important psychologically; it is the statutory rates that invite attention. Relaxing our assumptions, we can view the usual situation where exclusions are partial rather than general. Here the gain in incentive that might attend broadening the tax base would be a matter of spreading advantages more evenly. By eliminating what is now of special benefit to some people, all statutory rates and the effective rates for many taxpayers could be reduced. More than likely the full weight of the statutory scale will fall on increments and decrements contemplated in the decision to evade tax surreptitiously or to try to avoid burdens by getting an amendment through Congress. Devoting economic resources to tax avoidance is rightly criticized as highly wasteful and unpalatable. Favors for capital gains are supported on the ground that there would be dire economic consequences if full statutory rates were applied to this species of income. When critics argue that income taxes are too high, it is the statutory marginal rates that are cited to prove their case.

Returning to economic incentives, one can also argue that they

[22] The marginal rate in this context is but the ratio of taxes to income as applied to increments; with a progressive scale the marginal rate must always be higher than the effective rate.

are not adversely affected by high rates of any sort. In the case of taxes there are always two conflicting consequences for incentives. To put it in layman's terms, taxes discourage effort because they make the alternatives to effort relatively more attractive; they encourage effort because they make more of it necessary to achieve a customary or coveted standard of living. How these two conflicting tendencies balance out in specific situations is not deductively determinable. Levy questions whether on balance there is a clear case for the view that exemption changes have more impact on incentives than rate changes, other things being equal;[23] and indeed there is considerable empirical literature[24] which questions the impact of present income taxes on incentives to work. Vickrey acknowledges at least a *prima facie* case for the view that the better alternative from the point of view of incentive is low tax rates with low exemptions.[25] Suffice it to conclude with some reliance on common sense that if there is any merit at all in the widely acclaimed complaint that present taxes do hamper incentives, the rates are undoubtedly important in this unhappy result, and the statutory rates are somewhat more important in this respect than the effective rates.

The choice between rate changes and exemption changes has frequently been argued in the context of stabilization policy. The exemption-changes alternatives frequently have more effect on the progressivity of the tax system and thus more potency for affecting consumers' demand. Along with this positive change in progressivity, augmenting exemptions also adds to the built-in flexibility of the existing system, that is, it adds to the tendency for yields to fluctuate with changes in national income. Nevertheless rate changes appear to be the choice of most critics. The main reason is that the exemption level is thought to be politically less flexible than rate changes. If the former were raised during recession, it would be particularly difficult to reverse during prosperous times, especially

[23] *Op. cit.*, pp. 73–110.

[24] Well summarized in Earl R. Rolph and George F. Break, *Public Finance* (Ronald Press, 1961), Chap. 7.

[25] William Vickrey, "Rate Reduction or Increased Exemptions: The Economics of the Question," *Proceedings of the National Tax Association* (1954), p. 290; "Adjustment of Income Tax Schedules for Small Incomes," in U. S. Congress, Joint Committee on the Economic Report, *Federal Tax Policy for Economic Growth and Stability* (1955), pp. 347–52.

if such periods were attended by rising costs of living. In addition, rate changes are more readily incorporated into the practice of withholding.

Exemption Forms and Techniques

We have referred to four types of exemption techniques: continuing, initial, and vanishing exemptions, and tax credits. Before proceeding to further consideration of these devices, a fifth type must be introduced, namely, a percentage-of-income allowance.

Percentage-of-Income Allowance

Under this technique the absolute amount of exemptions increases as income advances; a simple application would allow a constant percentage of income as the latter moves upward. For instance, instead of the flat allowance of $600 for each dependent child, it might allow the taxpayer 5 percent of income. A minimum and/or maximum in absolute terms might be added.

This type of exemption recognizes the fact that well-to-do and wealthy families do not share their income with their children on the same absolute scale as the poor. (The kinship between this approach and the rationale of splitting may be noted.) It makes little sense to differentiate between a millionaire with dependents and another without them, so it is argued, by allowing the former $600, a mere bagatelle compared with what he may be expected to spend on a son or daughter. The case for percentage exemption is strongest in the case of dependents; an allowance of this sort for the taxpayer and spouse would be canceled out more largely by its generality and more readily converted to rate differentiation.

As is noted in the conference report, a percentage-of-income exclusion is a highly flexible instrument and one that can be used as a substitute for splitting or partial splitting.

It is hard to escape the conclusion that the percentage-of-income allowance is the rational culmination of the classical approach to ability to pay and its differentiation. However, the percentage allowance, at least in the upper brackets, makes no sense to those who view the purpose of the tax in this area as a case of controlling power. As previously observed, numbers (within families) are irrelevant to the power-dispensation philosophy.

Continuing Exemption

This is the system now used by the federal government and most of the states. It represents a compromise perhaps between the more logical techniques discussed above and the idea that exemptions should be confined to the underprivileged. It was inaugurated in Great Britain (for the standard tax) after long experience with the more limited type, probably in part to facilitate the transition between graduation by exemption and graduation by the rate structure. Its principal objection is that it discards a very large part of the potential tax base and throws the burden of revenue raising on very high marginal rates.

Initial and Vanishing Exemptions

The idea behind this type of exemption is to confine all or most of the benefit to the lower income classes that are excluded from paying any tax. As applied to the upper brackets of income it is in accord with the view that the family income is an index of its power, and the division of such income among family members is not significant. By the same token and from the classical point of view, it fails to supply needed differentiation among families except at the bottom of the scale.

As previously explained, the initial exemption carries with it a so-called notch problem, which the vanishing exemption seeks to avoid. Levy's book presents an intensive study of how this may be done without violating reasonable standards of good progression.[26] It may be added that, considering other compromises with strict standards of equity in the interest of simplicity (and to accommodate organized pressures?) which the law accepts, some rough approximations might be acceptable. Moreover, the range within which the device would operate is one where it would be practical to accommodate the taxpayer with a tax table.

A principal merit of the vanishing exemption is that it could add considerably to the tax base and/or finance a more generous scale of

[26] *Op. cit.*, pp. 11–26. An example is cited in note 19 to this chapter.

exclusions. Some rough calculations of these amounts based on 1959 data indicate that exemptions as presently applied on taxable returns cost the Treasury about $17.2 billion; that a vanishing exemption could be devised (with exemptions vanishing at the rate of $1 for every $4 by which adjusted gross income exceeds the present exemptions) that would save about $8.45 billion of this sum; and that this would finance a vanishing exemption beginning with $800 per capita with some $1.7 billion to spare.[27] It should be noted, however, that the vanishing exemption would have adverse distributional effects principally in the lower middle brackets and that this would call perhaps for an adjustment in rates that would be concentrated to some extent in this area.

Chart 1 shows the effective rate of tax under four types of exemption plans: $600 continuing, initial, and vanishing exemption and an 8-percent-of-income exemption.

The Income Tax Credit

As previously indicated, some states have substituted a tax credit for the more conventional income allowance in providing personal exemptions. For reasons previously discussed, continuing exemptions are more beneficial to the poor than to the rich, and they may accordingly be regarded as a progressive feature of the tax system. Nevertheless, in terms of tax-saving value, the flat allowance advances considerably with rising income. For instance, in the case of a taxpayer in the first bracket of income it is worth $120 per capita whereas for one paying at a marginal rate of 90 percent it is worth $540. The credit system commutes the tax-saving feature to a common value usually derived from the experience of the taxpayer in the lowest bracket. It is equivalent to an exemption which comes

[27] The estimates of revenue savings in using a vanishing exemption and the costs of expanding that exemption were computed on the following basis:

The dollar amount of the present $600 exemption in each adjusted gross income class for each of the five types of returns was subtracted from the adjusted gross income of each class to determine income available for vanishing. This provided a base against which to figure exemption deductions. An allowance was made for different patterns of exemptions within each income class. The reductions and exemptions as calculated were added back to the tax base. The proper marginal rate was then applied to the modified tax base. A similar procedure was repeated starting with an $800 per capita exemption instead of the present $600.

CHART 1. Effective Rates of Tax for a Family of Four with Different Exemption Plans

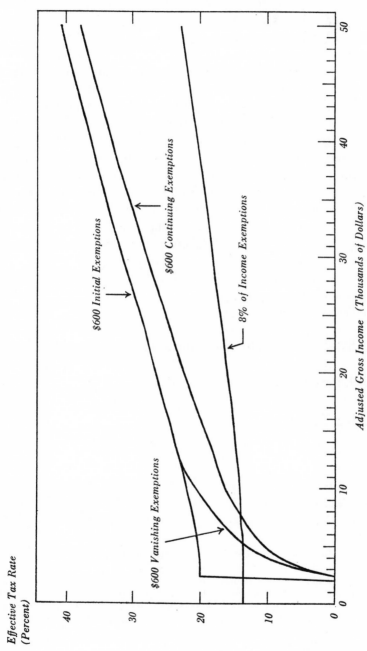

Assuming present rates and brackets with no deductions; vanishing exemption is reduced $1 for every $4 that adjusted gross income exceeds the basic exemption amount.

37

out of the bottom bracket rather than out of the top bracket. It may also be regarded as a vanishing exemption which never completely vanishes.[28] At the same time it avoids the notch problem, which attends initial exemptions.

Under several of the approaches that support exemptions the rationale of the income tax credit is weak. For instance, if it is assumed that clear income represents ability to pay and is the proper basis for differentiating among taxpayers, the credit makes no sense. It would be like applying the income tax rate to gross income before business expenses have been subtracted. Moreover, as compared with present practice it would collect relatively less revenue from smaller and more from larger families. In other words, it reduces differentiation for dependents especially in the higher brackets. But if it is assumed that exemptions should be confined in principle to the role of excluding low incomes from the tax base, it is at least an improvement over the income allowance.

If a credit tied to the first bracket[29] were substituted for the present federal exemption provision, the added revenue, according to our rough calculation, would be about $1.25 billion. Because returns and exemptions are heavily concentrated at the bottom of the taxable-income pyramid, the credit would mean a smaller saving in revenue than might be expected. Were the benefit of splitting removed, the effect would be much sharper.

Specific Problems

Among the more specific exemption problems which might command our attention are present special concessions to students (or parents of students), and to the aged and the blind, and possible concessions to working wives. The last of these will be discussed in Chapter IV. The double exemptions for the aged and the blind are a

---

[28] Thus under our present scale of exemptions a $120 tax credit would be the equivalent of a $132 exemption at the top of the scale.

[29] The calculation might assume that beginning with a three-unit family the tax-value of an additional exemption should be derived in part from the second bracket, and so on. As a concession to the view that large families involve economies of scale and in accordance with general state practice, all exemptions in our calculation are assumed to come out of the lowest bracket.

part of a larger problem (and set of institutions) concerning the application of the tax system to elderly and retired people and will be considered independently in Chapter III. We shall also consider here the standard deduction, which may be regarded as an extension of the personal exemption system.

Students

The present rule, dating from 1954, provides that a parent may claim a dependent's exemption for a youth over 19 years of age if such offspring is a student (as defined) and if the parent contributes more than half of the youth's support. The dependent may earn more than $600, in which case he will file an independent return, on which he also may claim an exemption for himself. In this situation the student is in effect allowed a double exemption. A typical scholarship held by the student is ignored in determining source of support. A married student may claim an exemption for his spouse only if neither the husband nor the wife is claimed as an exemption by some other person.

The present rule superseded an earlier one, which drew the line on the exemption allowance not in terms of support but in terms of the student's earnings; the parents could not claim an exemption for the student if he earned more than $600. The old rule was criticized because of its notch problem effect; at the point of $600 earnings a few dollars additional for the student would cost the parents at least $120 in a lost exemption. This was said to be a capricious trap for the unwary and to involve unfortunate disincentive effects on students' earnings. It is hard to see how the present rule is much better in these respects, though by spending a little more of father's money (or stretching the support rule with some impunity in terms of administration), it is perhaps now easier to escape the statutory trap. At some cost in terms of complication, the trap could be eliminated through the use of some device similar to the vanishing exemption.

Objection to the student-exemption rule, however, is not confined to its notch-problem aspect. Some critics argue that it has an unhappy incidence among rich and poor families and that as an instrument to promote education (which presumably was one of its objectives), the device is poorly designed.

INCIDENCE. The typical cost of a year in college, not counting opportunity costs, is in the area of $1,500. A student can usually earn about $500 gross of living expenses during a summer vacation, and a large number at least duplicate this with a part-time job during the school year.[30] We are informed that this can be done by an ambitious and reasonably competent student without much loss in the quality of his school work. The balance of this student's support is frequently supplied by his parents. Unhappily he fails to qualify for a dependent's exemption because his parents do not provide at least half of his support. In the case of more affluent families where the student doesn't work at all or only during summer vacations, qualification for the special exemption is assured.

To make matters worse it is possible for an affluent parent to endow his son or daughter with property, income from which will cover nearly half of college expenses for the youth. In this case in addition to the two exemptions for parent and dependent, the income from the securities might be demoted from a high to a low bracket rate. The tax saving value of this arrangement could add up to more than the $1,500, which is the typical cost of a college education.[31]

Question may be raised too about the equity of ignoring scholarships in the support rule, especially since a scholarship is favored directly through the rule that exempts it as an honorarium or gratuity.[32] Thus the scholarship student has little to worry about but

[30] See Arnold Kotz, "The Employment of Students," *Monthly Labor Review*, Vol. 83 (July 1960), pp. 705–09. Studies at the University of Wisconsin (L. J. Lins, *Student Expenses and Sources of Income 1960–61 Academic Year* [University of Wisconsin, Madison Campus, 1961]) indicate that in the case of undergraduates more than 45 percent of the male students and more than 42 percent of the female students work during the school year, with median time at between 10 and 11 hours weekly at wages slightly in excess of $1 per hour. Median income from summer employment is $581 for males and $327 for females. The mean income of single *graduate* students including scholarships and assistantships and (small) contributions from parents is in the area of $2,500; that for married students about $4,500.

[31] Say the student spends $4,001, of which the parent contributes $2,000 indirectly and $2,001 directly; suppose the parent is paying tax on marginal income at a rate of 90 percent: the tax saving on the indirect contribution alone would be 90 percent of $600 claimed by the son as a personal exemption and 70 percent of the remaining $1,400 (taxed to the son at a marginal rate of 20 percent). This adds up to more than $1,500.

[32] Any amount received as a scholarship at an educational institution is not counted in determining whether the taxpayer furnished more than half the support; amounts received as awards in recognition of educational achievement are with some qualifications not taxable.

the pursuit of his education; very likely he will not need to seek a job; he pays no taxes on his scholarship money; and he eases his father's tax load. The working student pays taxes and disqualifies his father from an exemption.

No doubt Congress found itself in a dilemma in dealing with these problems. It sought to differentiate sharply between two tax-payers in, let us say, a middle bracket of income, one of whom is supporting three children in college, the other none. But in doing so, it couldn't avoid the unwanted consequence of giving a better break to the well-to-do family with three children in college than to the much poorer family with the same responsibilities.

PROMOTING EDUCATION BY MEANS OF TAX DEDUCTIONS. As previously suggested, the student exemption may have resulted from the desire of Congress to promote education by offering help to families with children to educate. The evidence supporting the need for such assistance is ample. It is recognized that the drop-out of a large proportion of students between high school and college, many of them of superior capacity, involves a substantial waste of potential manpower. Economic reasons are among the most important causes of the drop-out.

A Ford Foundation survey[33] shows that of a sample of families who "plan" to send their children to college only 25 percent have made *any* financial provision for the contingency. Many hope that their children will get scholarships, but few get them, and few scholarships cover the whole cost of school.

One study[34] found that in 1953 nearly 20 percent of all college students came from families whose annual incomes were under $3,000, and nearly 50 percent came from those whose incomes were below $6,000. (These are not the families who enjoy the bounty of the present extra income tax exemption.) Less than 8 percent were from families with incomes above $15,000.

In 1957[35] the President's Committee on Education Beyond the High School recommended that deductions or credits be allowed

[33] Elmo Roper and associates, *Parents' College Plans Study* (Ford Foundation, 1959), p. iii.

[34] Elmer V. Hollis and associates, *Cost of Attending College* (U. S. Department of Health, Education, and Welfare, 1957), p. 47.

[35] *Second Report to the President* (July 1957), p. 11.

under the federal income tax for costs of formal education beyond the high school. Some critics, however, responded with the now familiar slogan that the federal income tax base has suffered enough erosion.

PROPOSED SOLUTIONS. Looking especially at the unhappy incidence of the present legislation, C. Lowell Harriss[36] has suggested that to claim an extra exemption in the parent-student situation, the parent be obliged to add the son's income, above a small ($200) minimum, to his own. No doubt this would give more weight to the vertical equities discussed above. In all cases where the son earned more than $200, the value of the parents' exemption would be reduced, and the reduction would generally be greatest in the higher brackets. If the student's income amounted to $800 or more, the double exemption would have no value no matter what the parents' income. If the exemption were claimed, more would be added to the tax base than the exemption would subtract. In the fairly typical case where the son earns $700 and the parent supplies $800, and the parent is paying taxes at the marginal rate of 26 percent, the latter would still profit to the extent of $26 by claiming the double exemption. On the other hand, in the case of the poorest families where the student earns more than $800, there would be no gain from the double exemption whether or not the family contributed more than half of the student's support. And in the most affluent cases where the son earns nothing, the full benefit of the special exemption would still be available even though no double exemption would be involved. The vertical inequity is as much the result of the special exemption (for dependent students over 19 years of age) as it is of double exemption. No doubt there is a strong case for generally taxing the parent on the minor's property income if the parent is the source of the endowment. And the same rule might hold for earned income above a minimum with an option in this case allowing either the youth or the parent to pay the tax and to claim one exemption.

A case could be made for confining the exemption privilege to

[36] "Parent and Child—and Taxes: Some Problems in Dependency," *Tax Revision Compendium* (cited in note 1 to this Chapter), pp. 531–36.

the working student and giving him a double exemption as is now done for the aged and the blind. This is based on the rationale that it ill behooves the government to make working one's way through college any more difficult. In terms of human resources that can promote national goals, a double exemption for youth pursuing a college education makes much better sense than a double exemption for the aged.

It may also be noted that under a vanishing-exemption system the problem of vertical inequities would largely take care of itself no matter what the exemption plan for students. The problem is thus to some extent part of the larger one of differentiation for dependents among families in the higher brackets. Stated another way, it makes little sense to allow for dependents (at all levels) during infancy and adolescence and then to cut off the allowance at the time when the dependent is likely to be most burdensome financially to his parents.

The Standard Deduction

In some sense personal deductions as well as exemptions should be included in a treatment of family-income taxation since they are both concerned with the family's consumption obligations, and they are in the accounting line of subtractions leading from adjusted gross to taxable income. The deductions here considered are distinguished from those for business and professional expenses—the negative items that must be offset against the positive ones to arrive at an algebraic total which the economists call "net income" and which are referred to on the tax forms as "adjusted gross income." On the other hand, deductions may be viewed as essentially similar to other special provisions of the income tax which affect its base and tax distribution. The standard deduction especially is little more than an additional exemption, and we shall treat it here as such. This will allow us to ignore the many problems related to specific personal deductions.

The federal income tax law introduced the standard deduction in 1943. Along with ceilings it provides presently that any taxpayer may deduct 10 percent of his income in lieu of itemized deductions, up to a maximum of $500 for single persons and $1,000 for other taxpayers. This was added to the law in the interest of simplicity and to lighten the load of the auditing staff.

In the area to which it applies and is used, the standard deduction ignores the most important function of deductions, namely to differentiate. Critics accordingly have argued that the opportunity was passed up to build the concession into the rate scale and thus keep marginal rates at more reasonable levels. This could be done readily by allowing personal deductions only to the extent that they exceed 10 percent of adjusted gross income. The mathematics of relativity holds in taxation as it does in physics. A proportional allowance to everybody is equivalent to an allowance to nobody. It is true that like the present standard deduction this proposal would do no differentiating. But possibly this is not a serious defect. We are familiar with the fact that because everybody or nearly everybody incurs some medical expense, we allow a deduction only for those medical bills in excess of 3 percent of adjusted gross income. Similarly everybody gives, or should give, a little of his income to his favorite church or charity, and nearly everybody has some state and local taxes to pay. X may have one type of deduction and Y another, but in the usual experience they add up to some modest proportion of income. There are exceptions, of course, and these are recognized by the privilege of itemizing and deducting if the sum for the individual taxpayer exceeds the average. Attention should be called to the fact that unless exemptions were simultaneously increased, the proposal would mean that families with income of less than $667 per member, who now pay no income tax, would be obliged to pay a tax. The standard deduction in effect, increases the personal-exemption exclusion by $67.

The idea of allowing deductions only in excess of a specified percentage of income could be applied not only to replace the standard deduction but also in the case of particular deductions. Since state and local taxes as a percentage of income do not vary widely either among taxpayers of different income levels or among those at the same level, it would seem to be particularly feasible to build much of their deductibility into the rate scale.[37] Protection against con-

[37] C. Harry Kahn, *Personal Deductions in the Federal Income Tax* (National Bureau of Economic Research, Princeton University Press, 1960), p. 100.

fiscation and the hazards of interstate competition[38] could be largely preserved by the simple rule that either taxes themselves or total deductions be allowed for exclusion only to the extent that they exceed a certain percentage of income.

Summary and Conclusion

In our discussion of income tax exemptions the following points stand out as worthy of recapitulation:

1. Exemptions and graduation are in large part exchangeable phenomena accomplishing the same objectives; and use of graduation rather than exemptions offers the considerable advantage of lower statutory marginal rates.

2. In terms of equity, exemptions are defended on the ground that the sacrifice associated with a subsistence minimum is not commensurate with other sacrifices the taxpayer is asked to bear; they are also defended on the ground that clear income rather than net income provides the fairest basis for differentials in tax distribution. However, under a socio-economic approach, stressing power rather than sacrifice, differentiation according to size of family is required only at the bottom of the scale.

3. As to size of exemptions, our system departs substantially at several points from the conclusions of budgetary studies of the cost of living. Viewed in absolute terms, deficiencies may be defended on the ground of revenue need and the civic desirability of wide participation in direct taxation. Viewed in relative terms, the departures are more vulnerable, but even here some rational defense can be offered to defend them. We conclude that the case against our present per capita system is not a clear and compelling one.

4. A strong case can be made, however, for the idea of vanishing exemptions, which would seek to use the exemption institution mainly to exclude certain taxpayers below a minimum level of income from paying any tax; or for a tax credit which moves in the same direction less rigorously. Either would serve to conserve the tax

[38] See the testimony on this subject before the House Ways and Means Committee, especially that of Melvin I. White and Harvey E. Brazer (cited in note 1 to this Chapter), pp. 365–418.

base and throw more weight on graduation to achieve differentiation. Another means to this same end would be to break up the first income bracket into several components taxed at much lower rates than the present one. However, vanishing exemptions or credits could also provide the revenue to finance more generous exclusions, and this is in accord with the view that any taxation at these levels is costly in terms of social objectives and at odds with welfare programs that underwrite a minimum.

5. The special exemption for students (or their parents), like some other income tax concessions, probably adds more to vertical inequity than it contributes to horizontal equity. A double exemption for *working* students would seem in several respects a more suitable means to serve the objectives of the present law.[39]

6. The standard deduction, allowed in terms of a flat percentage of income, is little more than an addition to the personal exemption, and it is one that could readily be built into the rate scale thus closing in some degree the gap between adjusted gross and taxable income.

[39] For other suggested improvements, see the conference report, pp. 93–108.

CHAPTER III

Tax Treatment of the Aged and Blind

THE APPLICATION of the income tax to the aged and the blind raises several issues that call for special consideration. This chapter deals principally with the special provisions affecting the aged: (1) special treatment of retirement income; (2) retirement-income credit; (3) double exemption for the elderly taxpayer and spouse; and (4) special provision for deduction of expenses for medical care.

The Aged

The special treatment of retirement income involves the exclusion of social security and railroad retirement benefits from the income tax base at the time of their receipt. Since employees' contributions to these programs are not deductible, some part of the beneficiaries' receipts may be regarded as having been taxed once when paid. However, social security payments can also be regarded as a transfer from the present young to the present old, and it is a well-known fact that at least the present generation of beneficiaries has contributed only a very minor part of what it is receiving.[1] No matter how social security benefits are visualized, employers' con-

---

[1] One authority calculates that as of 1960 only about 5 percent of social security benefits had been "prepaid." This includes both employees' contributions and those paid by employers on employees' behalf (Frank G. Dickinson, "The Social Security Principle," *The Journal of Insurance*, Vol. 27 [December 1960], p. 7).

tributions currently and when paid to beneficiaries later escape the base entirely.[2]

The retirement income tax credit inaugurated in 1954 aimed at parity privileges for those not covered by social security. It provides a tax credit not to exceed the tax on $1,524 of income at the first bracket rate—a maximum of $304.80. Interest, dividends, and rent qualify for the credit as does the portion of private pensions and annuities currently taxable. However, the receipt of social security or railroad retirement benefits or of earned income above certain limits disqualifies the taxpayer for use of the credit or reduces the base. If the taxpayer is over 72, he is not obliged to reduce the base of the credit regardless of the amount earned. Between ages 65 and 72 he must reduce the base 50 cents for each dollar earned over $1,200 and not exceeding $1,700, and dollar for dollar thereafter.

The double exemption for the elderly provides simply that after reaching age 65 the taxpayer may exclude $1,200 of otherwise taxable income instead of the usual $600, and he may do the same for his spouse (if she is also over 65 years of age). On qualifying joint returns this adds up to an exclusion of $2,400.

The usual medical-care-expense deduction provides for the subtraction of medical expenses in excess of 3 percent of adjusted gross income (in excess of 1 percent for the cost of medicine and drugs). Ceilings are provided: $5,000 on a separate return, $10,000 on a joint return, an additional $5,000 for dependents, and an overall ceiling of $20,000. (Before 1962 each of these figures was half of the

[2] Retirement income also includes private pension benefits and private annuities and several other categories which we are unable here to discuss in any detail. Employers' contributions to private pension funds which qualify under the code are deductible to them. These contributions are not taxed immediately to the employees, and the interest on these funds which accumulates to the individual's account is also excluded from immediate taxation. The tax on these elements is deferred until the beneficiary receives his benefits during retirement. His own contributions, being currently nondeductible, are taxed as earned, and these are treated as a return of capital or savings as received. The treatment of a private annuity is similar except that in this case the only deferral of tax obligations is on the interest accruing to the personal contributions of the beneficiary. In both cases special rules that have changed over the years govern the separation of previously taxed returned savings and the untaxed portion that the pensionee or annuitant must include on his tax returns as his retirement program pays off. The treatment of personal direct saving, investment, and dissaving to finance retirement differs mainly in that in this case there is no deferment of tax on interest and/or dividends as the funds accumulate.

**TABLE 2. Estimated Money Income of Tax Units
With at Least One Spouse Over 65, in 1960[a]**

(In billions of dollars)

Source of Income		Amount
Income Maintenance Programs		14.1
OASDI	8.2	
Railroad Retirement	0.6	
Other Public Retirement	1.9	
Public Assistance	1.9	
Total Public Plans	12.6	
Private Plans	1.5	
Wages and Salaries		11.1
Others (Dividends, rent, interests, business, etc.)		15.8
Total		41.0

[a] The following limitations to the above figures should be noted: (1) An upward adjustment of 10 percent for unreported wages and salaries has been made to the amounts reported for tax purposes; (2) the private pension plans amount is only that reported on tax returns; (3) the "other" income has been adjusted upward for nontaxable capital gains but does not reflect nontaxable dividends and interest nor any amounts in this category not reported on tax returns.

In addition, the table does not reflect funds available from liquidation of assets, nonmoney incomes, and payments made by other agencies or persons either in cash to the aged or for services to the aged.

The data is derived primarily from Social Security Administration reports and the 1960 Statistics of Income.

present allowances.) If the taxpayer or spouse is age 65 or over, the 3 percent rule (but not the 1 percent rule for drugs) is waived. The maximum limitations are also more generous. If either the taxpayer or his spouse is over 65 *and* disabled, the maximum allowed is $20,000; and if both spouses are disabled and over 65 years of age, the maximum is $40,000.

Economic Circumstances of the Aged

As of 1958, Wilbur J. Cohen[3] calculated that the total money income of the aged was in the area of $25 to $30 billion dollars. Computations for 1960 indicate a total figure of approximately $41 billion (see Table 2), with roughly two-thirds of this being conceptually gross income as defined by the tax laws. In 1960, $24.3 billion

[3] "Income and Tax Status of the Aged: Present Situation and Possible Modifications of Existing Policies," testimony submitted to the House Committee on Ways and Means, *Tax Revision Compendium*, Vol. 1 (November 1959), pp. 539–50.

was reported as adjusted gross income, $20.5 billion of this being on taxable returns. Taxes paid total $3.67 billion before credits and $3.46 billion after credits.

As to distribution, Eveline Burns testified before the Ways and Means Committee[4] that in 1956 and 1957, three-fifths of all people aged 65 and over had incomes of less than $2,000. In 1957 "the median total income of retired beneficiary couples [under OASI] was $2,249, and the median amount of independent income other than OASI was $595 for those with such income and $158 for the group as a whole (including the 31.5 percent who had no income other than OASI)."[5] She concluded that the double exemption privilege cannot be a significant aid to many people.

On the other hand, some evidence indicates that a significant proportion of elderly couples are well-to-do and probably a dispro-portionately high percentage of the very wealthy are elderly peo-ple.[6] We know less than we should about life-patterns of income. One study concluded with the generalization that great diversity attends the economic status of elderly citizens with the retirement of a substantial number and the continued high salary and/or receipts from capital of another large group.[7] Some evidence that at all ages financial assistance flows predominantly from parents to children rather than the reverse supports this view.

Tax critics join those of old age benefits in finding much to criticize in the institutions described above. A simple general pre-scription to which many might subscribe would be the elimination of all of them.

Exclusion of OASI and Railroad Retirement Income

According to Dan Smith the exclusion "was the result of a ruling which may not have been well reasoned, given shortly after the

[4] "Taxation of the Aged: Retirement Income Credit and the Like," *ibid.*, pp. 551–58.

[5] *Ibid.*, p. 553.

[6] See for instance Lampman's data on wealth-holding by age groups (Robert J. Lampman, *The Share of Top Wealth-Holders in National Wealth* [National Bureau of Economic Research, Princeton University Press, 1962], pp. 17–21).

[7] Janet Fisher, "Income, Spending, and Saving Patterns of Consumer Units in Different Age Groups," *Studies in Income and Wealth* (National Bureau of Economic Research, 1952).

social security system was established."[8] He adds the opinion that "the taxation of old age social security benefits should have been adopted at the time the double personal exemption was granted in 1948. This was recommended in the report of the Staff of the Joint Committee on Internal Revenue Taxation, but it was not done apparently because the double exemption was sufficiently generous to make most social security benefits nontaxable anyway."

It is true that social security allowances are meager enough for some people and understandable that legislators might wish to amplify the pension system with income tax favors. The critics hold that the inadequacy of benefits can be managed more precisely and economically by direct measures. One could argue that a tax on the government's own bounty is a case of taking money out of one pocket and putting it into another. This philosophy was at one time applied to the interest on federal bonds, but it was abandoned as to new issues after 1940. A good working rule widely accepted among tax critics is that for the purpose of a graduated income tax, the base should be universal in its coverage. If exceptions are allowed, they should carry a high burden of proof. The present rule loses for the tax base employers' contributions, any interest which a reserve may accumulate, and the portion of the benefit which is in the nature of a subsidy.

Of course, it must be recognized that current payments by employees are nondeductible and that to tax social security benefits in full without changing this feature would involve an element of double taxation. The simple way to avoid this would be to make such contributions deductible. This would eliminate the injustice for those who contribute to the system but for one reason or another fail to get anything out of it. An alternative and much more complicated (but theoretically correct) procedure would be to treat social security benefits like those from a private annuity and exclude the portion estimated to have been contributed by the beneficiary. A third alternative would be to treat the employer's contribution as income in kind (fringe benefit) to the employee when payments are made on his behalf. Such payments, however, give no fully vested interest to anybody. It can be argued that taxes are harder to pay

[8] Dan Throop Smith, *Federal Tax Reform* (McGraw-Hill, 1961), p. 85.

during the financial strain of old age. But graduated rates and (even ordinary) exemptions already accommodate this circumstance.

Retirement Income Tax Credit

The retirement income tax credit, as was previously explained, was designed as a consolation to those not covered by social security, and its usefulness has waned as the coverage of the system has expanded dramatically. Of course, if social security benefits had been taxable at the beginning, there never would have been any excuse for this complication that brings so little relief to very few people. Ethel Perry Andrus submitted the following evidence to the Ways and Means Committee in 1959: "On 1955 returns only 17 percent of total retirement income reported by the elderly taxpayers was eligible for retirement income credit."[9] She concluded that the retirement credit was not available to those who need it most. She concluded further that the credit would be more effective it if were augmented. But, as previously suggested, the more popular solution (among the critics) would be to get rid of the credit entirely. Hardly any modification could do more for simplicity at lesser cost to equity. It takes two-thirds of a page on the tax form to instruct the taxpayer on how to compute the credit.

The Double Exemption for Aged Couples

The most rational defense for this provision would be evidence that the aged encounter especially heavy living expenses. Unfortunately for its proponents, budget studies show that this is not the case. They show that in general it costs less to live at a given standard after one reaches retirement age than before.[10] This is not to deny of course that large numbers of people are obliged to live on less income after retirement than they had before. To this the an-

[9] "Taxation of the Aged," *Tax Revision Compendium* (cited in note 3 to this Chapter), p. 570.

[10] *Monthly Labor Review* (November 1960), p. 1198, presents budget studies by age and indicates that a couple age 65 and over will incur approximately 6 percent less cost in maintaining a given standard of living than a couple within the age range of 35 to 65 years. The study deals with "modest but adequate" budgets and covers the twenty largest cities.

swer is given that graduated rates and ordinary exemptions are the proper accommodation of tax burdens to different levels of income—whether between two persons at the same age or one person at different ages. We know too little about life-cycle patterns of income distribution to adjust taxes to age levels with any pretense of adhering to a standard of equity. Moreover, the double allowance system passes over the heads of those who need it most.

Special Allowances for Medical Care Expense

This appears to be the easiest to defend of the tax institutions designed to help the aged. The special vulnerability of the aged to medical bills of catastrophic proportion is well known. It constitutes a defense only for the higher ceilings allowed the aged in medical expense deduction, and even here it is perhaps more logical to attack the ceilings generally. However, it can be shown that the aged find casualty insurance expensive and difficult to procure, and the coverage among older people is limited.

But here again the deduction does nothing for elderly people who would pay no income tax even without it. "Of a total of 1.22 million returns from persons 65 or over claiming the deduction in 1956, 464,000 were from persons with incomes of $5,000 or more."[11] Returns for 1956 indicate that only 147,000 persons over 65 filing returns with incomes under $2,000 claimed the medical deduction. Just over 115,000 returns were nontaxable returns. Social insurance for the aged via medical care deductions is thus, to say the least, very spotty.

Some Generalizations on Tax Privileges for the Aged

The whole area we have been discussing provides an excellent case study of special exclusions from the income tax and lends support to the following generalizations:

1. Assuming a minimum tax-free allowance of some sort to start with, the only way to help the most underprivileged is to give positive assistance rather than negative concessions under the income tax. The income tax is not a universal tax, and concessions

[11] Burns, *op. cit.*, p. 554.

made under it can be of no benefit to those whose incomes are so low that they would not be taxed even without the concession. Yet in many cases it is sympathy for these submarginal individuals which prompts the concession. Particularly conspicuous in the field we are considering is a combination of privileges, piled one upon another, which are obviously surplus for many older people in need and which greatly reduce the tax of those who are in no sense underprivileged.

2. A blanket exclusion that applies alike to the affluent and the indigent among a large class of taxpayers is likely to give undue advantage to certain of the rich, both as compared with other rich and as compared with the poor. In short, the exclusions are a blunt instrument and do an undiscriminating job. The graduated rate is a discriminator of no little capacity and precision, and exclusions are likely to interfere seriously with its natural role in this regard.

The provisions we have been discussing undoubtedly do produce a maze of unwanted unneutralities both horizontal and vertical. A couple receiving maximum benefit under the Railroad Retirement System might get as much as $5,744.40 and pay no taxes at all!

There are unneutralities too among the beneficiaries of various retirement programs. The Railroad Retirement System grants more generous benefits and therefore larger exclusions from income tax than does OASI. The double exemption for spouses allows an aged couple to live very much better free of tax than can a single person, and so on.

3. Where special favors are introduced via exclusions into a graduated income tax system, they invite others to compensate for inequities generated by the first departure.

4. In general, government subsidies if they are to be introduced into the economic system should be taxed. An effort to amplify the subsidies via tax exemption leads to unwanted consequences.

The Blind

The principal rational defense for a double exemption for the blind lies in budgetary studies showing that the blind must incur higher expenses than do others to live at a given standard. One thinks at once of the need to procure and maintain guide dogs, various reading aids, transportation with guides, and so on. However, much of this is available to the blind directly and without cost from state and federal agencies and/or programs designated especially for this purpose. Of course, these concessions are not taxable. Welfare budgets usually mention some extra allowances for the blind because of higher general living expenses, but they are relatively minor. There are other classes of disabled persons with special needs. Many of the blind are above age 65 and qualify for double exemption independently of blindness. Only a minor proportion are gainfully employed. However academic the conclusion, the evidence appears mainly to support the view that this is another area in which a sensitive society should grant generous assistance, but that a double exemption in the tax laws is not the appropriate way to do it.

CHAPTER IV

Income Splitting

THE INSTITUTION OF INCOME SPLITTING, as applied in the United States, starts with the aggregate income of spouses; this is then halved, the tax is based on this figure, and the tax as thus computed is then multiplied by two to determine the total tax for the couple. The issue is associated with progressive taxation and would be of little or no importance under a proportional tax. With a common schedule for married and unmarried taxpayers, splitting automatically widens the bracket limits for married couples and thus reduces the applicable progressive rates. In the application of a graduated income tax to the family, splitting shares the center of the stage with the personal exemption system.

The institution of splitting poses two main issues: (1) What is the proper unit among various family situations for assessing a graduated tax?[1] and (2) What relative taxes should married couples and single persons with the same taxable incomes pay?

As to the assessment unit, there are four main possibilities. They are: (1) the individual; (2) the husband and wife (marital unit); (3) the family (spouses and minor children); and (4) the household (including those living in a common household).

---

[1] It is useful to distinguish the assessment unit from the tax-filing unit and the tax-paying unit. The federal government now allows splitting only in the case of joint returns, and the liability as between spouses is joint and several. Other arrangements are possible.

The issue of relative burdens arises only if a unit larger than the individual is chosen as a basis for comparison. Obviously if all taxpayers were single, no problem of family tax treatment would arise; and if the choice were to disregard family relations and treat everybody as independent entities, the problem would be avoided though perhaps at high cost in terms of equity. Again there are two possibilities: mandatory joint returns and the split-income plan. (A dual-rate schedule can be used to accomplish either.) Under so-called mandatory joint returns, the incomes of the members of the unit are aggregated, and the rate scale is applied to the base. A married couple (or family) and a single person with equal *taxable* income pay the same tax. The technique of the split-income plan has been explained above. It may be applied to spouses only or to the entire family including children. In the former case a married couple pays taxes at the same rate as a single person with one-half their income.

The dual-rate plan provides a separate schedule of rates and/or brackets for single persons, married couples, and perhaps for families of varying sizes. Two plans of this character which have received considerable attention in the United States and which afford a sharp contrast are those associated with the names of Joseph A. Pechman and William Vickrey. The Pechman plan[2] would allow couples to split their income for tax purposes but would eliminate the advantage by halving the brackets for married persons. In terms of distribution of the tax load, it would be very similar to mandatory joint returns. Vickrey, who wrote on the subject before the passage of the 1948 legislation, would disallow splitting on joint returns and would halve the brackets for married persons filing separate returns and single taxpayers.[3] This would distribute the tax burden much as the split-income plan would. The plan also avoids controversy about penalizing married persons. (This will be dis-

[2] Joseph A. Pechman, "Income Splitting," testimony submitted to the House Committee on Ways and Means, *Tax Revision Compendium*, Vol. 1 (November 1959), pp. 473–86.

[3] William Vickrey, *Agenda for Progressive Taxation* (Ronald Press, 1947), pp. 274–87. Thus, using present rates, single people and married taxpayers filing separate returns according to the present scale would pay on taxable income as follows: on the first $2,000, 20 percent; on the second, 22 percent; on the third, 26 percent; and so on. Married people filing joint returns would pay on their combined taxable income as follows: On the first $4,000, 20 percent; on the second, 22 percent, and so on.

CHART 2. Effective Rates of Tax at Various Levels of Taxable Income
Present, Vickrey and Pechman Plans

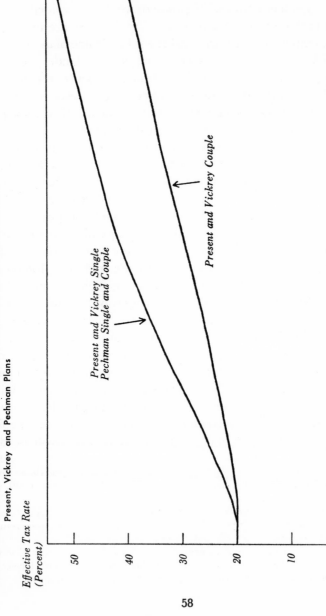

Effective Tax Rate
(Percent)

Present and Vickrey Single
Pechman Single and Couple

Present and Vickrey Couple

Taxable Income   (Thousands of Dollars)

cussed further below.) The controversial point in it as in income splitting is the advantage it gives to married over single taxpayers.

The relationships of burdens under the above mentioned proposals are depicted in Chart 2 starting from present rates. It should be noted that relative burdens are the principal issue at stake and that absolute burdens are adjustable to revenue needs and the degree of progression desired. The Vickrey plan would have increased the burden on married couples where both spouses have an income (as compared with pre-1948), but it would avoid the consequence of their marrying into higher brackets under the new schedules.

Our problem is further complicated by the fact that married couples with the same aggregate incomes are not a homogeneous group; in some cases one spouse earns all the money income, and in others both spouses "work" and receive wages. It can be argued plausibly that the two groups differ in terms of imputed income, extra expense, security, greater prestige associated with one well-paying job than with two less renumerative positions, penalty against marriage, and so on.

The problem may be presented concretely in terms of four family taxable-income situations: The Whites and Blacks both have taxable aggregate family incomes of $8,000, but Mr. White alone provides for the Whites; in the case of the Blacks the family support comes equally from the two spouses. Blue and Green are two single individuals with taxable incomes of $8,000 and $4,000 respectively. Should the Blacks and Whites contribute equally, and if so, should they pay as much as Blue or only twice as much as Green? It will be noted that by stating the problem in terms of taxable income we have abstracted from related problems of relative exemptions and deductions. However, it should be added that manipulating these collateral institutions, as in the case of child-care expense, is a possible solution to the problem.

Background

It is probably fair to say that the income tax and estate and gift tax amendments of 1948 were a political compromise dictated by a high-pressure historical situation and that they were hardly a deliberate choice made after all the equities and other consequences were weighed. A considerable part of the credit or discredit for the amendments can be attributed to the United States Supreme Court.

State Property Tax Law and United States Supreme Court Decisions

The story begins with the property tax law of the states, which became the basis of the federal income tax law as applied to the family. Most of the states derived their property law from England, where it had developed as a feature of the common law. However, the law of equity and statute law mitigated the harshness of the common law and placed a married woman on an equal basis with her husband in the ownership of property. Nevertheless, the basis of ownership continued to be individualistic, depending on the active role of the spouse in acquiring income or property. The intangible ingredient of inspiration contributed by the inactive spouse was never recognized in legal terms—not until a few states broke with precedent under the spur of federal tax incentives shortly before 1948.

A few of the states took their property law from Spain. This so-called "community property law" recognized an equal claim of the spouses to income attributable directly or indirectly to the efforts of either partner after marriage. The original community property states were California, Louisiana, Texas, Idaho, Washington, Arizona, Colorado, Nevada, and New Mexico. As indicated above, several other states later made a bid for tax advantages by copying the law of the original nine states. Oklahoma started this movement, and a motivating factor was conceded to be the desire to prevent an exodus of wealthy oil men to nearby Texas. Oregon, Michigan, Nebraska, and Pennsylvania then joined the movement and further undermined the old structure of joint and separate returns. One writer, referring to legal splitting, said that formerly "it was respectable, and tax avoidance existed not in its origin but in its results."[4]

Early federal statutes apparently levied taxes on income according to title as determined by state property law. In 1921 the Attorney General ruled that husband and wife could each report half of community property in all the so-called community property states except California. The California situation started a wave of litiga-

---

[4] Stanley S. Surrey, "Family Income and Federal Taxation," *Taxes*, Vol. 24 (October 1946), p. 982.

tion beginning with *United States v. Robbins*[5] in 1925. The first decision went against the taxpayer, based in part on the special feature in the state under which the vested interest of the wife was only an expectation. But Justice Holmes for the Court went further to note and rest his opinion mainly on the point that the husband had full power of disposition of the entire income. This seemed to say that it was the practical rights of ownership or control that should be determining rather than the formalities of title. However, in *Poe v. Sanborn* (1930),[6] Justice Roberts established the rule that ownership rather than control should be the test. The opposite rule of the *Robbins* case was applied in trust and assignment issues. Thus if A assigns his wages to his son B, the fact that B takes title does not absolve A; and the same is true in many cases where A sets up a trust for B, especially if the duration of the trust is short and/or A retains important elements of control. California amended its law to avoid the effects of the *Robbins* decision.

Thus the Supreme Court laid the ground for the problem of geographic inequity, which was later to force a revision in the assessment unit. At the time of the *Poe* decision the federal tax was a relatively mild one with conservative graduation of rates. During the subsequent years, and particularly during World War II, there were drastic increases in the severity of the law, creating conspicuous and intolerable advantages for many taxpayers in the community property states. The evidence indicates that the beneficiaries in community property states were not numerous, but that the benefits they received, which varied according to bracket, were in some cases very substantial.

Meanwhile the Court had also raised doubts concerning the constitutionality of mandatory joint returns. Wisconsin's first income tax provided for a family return including not only the income of the husband and wife (living together) but also that of children under 18 years of age. Moreover, the husband was made liable for the total tax. An amendment in 1925 dispersed the liability among family members according to their respective shares in the total family income. The law was challenged and sustained in the state court but ruled out on appeal to the national tribunal. Wisconsin

[5] 269 U. S. 315 (1925).
[6] 282 U. S. 101 (1930).

thereupon restored a system of separate returns, which it has continued to the present time.

Justice Roberts for the Court[7] stated that "any attempt by a state to measure the tax on one person's property or income by reference to the property or income of another is contrary to due process of law." He added: "It can hardly be claimed that a mere difference in social relation so alters the taxable status of one receiving income as to justify a different measure." Justice Holmes (joined by Justices Brandeis and Stone) for the minority argued that the state's authority to regulate marriage implied the power to tax accordingly; that the state may in its classification take account of the normal pooling of family resources and of the susceptability of a tax to evasion.

Since the *Hoeper* case and the *Poe* case the tendency in court laws as in legislation is to give priority to economic criteria in tax matters over the technical tests of local property law. Moreover, two Puerto Rican court decisions[8] have sustained joint-return statutes; and petitions for writs of certiorari were denied by United States courts. That the family is a closely related financial unit has frequently been noted in avoidance cases. The split-income plan itself uses the family unit as a basis for graduation; income is pooled (with title disregarded) prior to splitting. Students of public finance with few exceptions regard the family rather than the individual as the proper unit for income taxation.

Other Cause for Action in 1948

Although the inequities of splitting under state law did not exist in the common law states, another type of inequity was making its appearance there. It consisted of various legal devices by which property and income from property could be divided between spouses (and other family members) in most cases without dividing control. Among them were: (1) direct gifts of income-producing property; (2) joint ownership of property; (3) family partnerships; and (4) family trusts. The direct assignment of income was early

---

[7] *Hoeper v. Tax Commission of Wisconsin*, 284 U. S. 214 (1930).

[8] *Ballester v. Court of Tax Appeals*, 61 PRR 460 (1943); *D'Imperior v. Sec. of Treas.*, 76 PRR 302 (1953); reviewed and sustained by U. S. Circuit Courts, 142 F. 2nd 11 (1944); 223 F. 2nd 413 (1955).

ruled out in the case of *Lucas v. Earl*,[9] in which Justice Holmes enlisted the oft-quoted figurative phrase that the fruit must be attributed to the tree on which it grew. The Court kept a close vigil on the use of devices of this sort, but it was hard put to prevent a considerable traffic in this area. The unneutralities resulting were largely between property income and earned income. They provided the second, and no doubt minor, cause for action in 1948.

Legislative History

Long before events of the late 1940's there had been proposals in or to the Congress aimed at mitigation of unneutral splitting. The earliest ones have been described as "management and control plans." Following the principles enunciated in the *Lucas* and *Robbins* cases, they proposed to tax community income to the spouse who exercised management and control over the community property. A bill of this type was first recommended to Congress by the Secretary of the Treasury in 1921, and numerous others were introduced in later years up to 1941, some of them passing one house of Congress. These plans were directed solely at the community property states, and they were vehemently and eloquently opposed by representatives and witnesses from these areas. Opponents argued, among other points, for the states' traditional sovereignty in property matters and claimed that community property was a sound bulwark of women's rights. It was also argued that the proposed approach would do nothing to check more subtle avoidance in the common law states.

Mandatory joint returns were also frequently proposed. It was and is the traditional British institution, and it was used in the pioneering Wisconsin statute of 1911. Important hearings were held in 1942, when the Treasury repeated its proposal for a mandatory joint return, with some concession for earned income to which both spouses contributed. The main arguments of the opposition were that the plan would damage women's rights and that it would promote divorce and illegitimate cohabitation. Whatever its merits, this line of argument had a wide popular appeal. One witness argued[10] "that taxation on a basis that distinguishes between her as

[9] 281 U. S. 111 (1930).
[10] *Revenue Revision of 1942*, Hearings before the House Committee on Ways and Means, 77 Cong. 2 sess., p. 1288.

married and as unmarried, is discriminatory and contrary to the spirit of the Married Women's Property Act." The Ways and Means Committee replied to this argument as follows: "The inherent property rights of the separate members of the taxable unit are in no way invalidated. The proposal merely determines the amount of tax to be paid by the unit and permits the tax so determined to be apportioned on an equitable basis. . . . It is not believed that the joint return will result in any increase in the divorce rate in the United States. A compulsory joint return has been required . . . in Great Britain and their divorce rate is not as high as in the United States."[11]

During the considerable amount of debate in the 1940's dual-rate-schedule plans received only informal and superficial consideration.

The successful proposal and now the federal law was the split-income plan, under which married taxpayers filing a joint return might compute the tax on one-half the aggregate income and multiply this figure by two to get the total tax. The idea was proposed in Great Britain as early as 1916 by Sidney Webb[12] and was mentioned favorably by Professor Carl Shoup in the United States in 1940.[13] Stanley Surrey in a speech before the National Association of Manufacturers in 1946 advocated the plan,[14] and it was soon espoused by that organization, the American Bar Association, the United States Chamber of Commerce, and the Committee for Economic Development. The Treasury never stated its opinion of the principle of splitting income though it disapproved of the cost in terms of revenue. Several former supporters of mandatory joint returns transferred their allegiance to the split-income plan when it became apparent that the former plan was politically unfeasible.

In 1947 a split-income amendment was included as a feature of two tax reduction bills, both of which passed the Congress and were vetoed by the President. It was attempted again in 1948, and a new feature was added to repeal the 1942 estate and gift tax amendments, about which more will be said below. Suffice it here to say

[11] *Revenue Revision of 1941*, Report by the House Committee on Ways and Means, 77 Cong. 1 sess., pp. 14–22.

[12] *How to Pay for the War* (London: Fabian Society, 1916), p. 258.

[13] "Married Couples Compared with the Single Person Under the Income Tax," *Bulletin of National Tax Association*, Vol. 25 (February 1940).

[14] Reprinted in *Taxes* (cited in note 4 to this Chapter).

that this feature of the bill won a great deal of support from the community-property states, which had initially been opposed to the split-income plan. With this support, the bill was passed and sustained over the President's veto.

The popularity of the measure in and out of Congress is not hard to explain. Several states had changed to the community property system of law; others had threatened to do so, and the pressure for "reform" was very great. The system reduced taxes for the middle- and upper middle-income classes without disturbing rates and without any absolute increase in the taxes of other groups. The estate and gift tax concession was successfully calculated to interest representatives from the community property states. The Congress (though not the President) was convinced that the time was appropriate for tax relief. The historical conjunction of a desire for tax relief and the critical community property problem accounts in large part for what seems to many an extraordinary product.

Estate and Gift Tax Development

Up to 1942 the division of community property required no gift tax. Differences between the community property states and other states also developed in the application of the estate tax. The husband on his death was taxed on only half of the community property held by him and his wife. Under an amendment enacted in 1942, economic origin of property was substituted for legal ownership as the criterion of taxability. This was in open defiance of local property law and was an invitation to follow the same course in dealing with the similar income tax problem. However, when the wife died first, her property was subject to tax on the theory that she had the testamentary right to dispose of her share of the community property. This inconsistency caused considerable resentment in the community property states. The gift tax was modified to follow consistently the economic source.

The 1948 law supplied a new approach fully recognizing community property for estate and gift tax purposes and giving comparable privileges to spouses in noncommunity-property states. It extended to death taxes, privileges parallel to those allowed in the income tax. Thus the "marital deduction" feature of the estate and gift tax was born. One-half the gift of a married person was considered to come from his spouse. The splitting of estates thus invited results in lower marginal rates and a doubling of exemptions. This is in addition to the fact that the gift tax carries lower rates than the estate tax, adding to the tax advantage of life-time transfers. The ultimate in splitting for the death tax is a four-way split as follows: one-quarter may be given to a son directly and during life; another quarter may be given indirectly (as presumed) through the spouse; a third quarter may be left to the spouse by testamentary transfer (she presumably will later bequeath this to the heir); and a fourth quarter may be left to the heir again by testamentary transfer. "For those who contemplate a career in the legal profession, the estate tax cannot be overlooked lightly; it is a highly remunerative field of practice and one in which bad advice can cost clients heavily."[15]

Experience of American States and Foreign Countries

As of 1961 a majority of income tax states use the optional joint and separate return system (as did the federal government before 1948), but ten states have followed the late federal law of income-splitting. However, all of these latter states except two are community property states. Eight states require that the parent include the income of minor children with his own for tax purposes. This is in accord with the rule of law in both the community property and the common law states. The record does not reveal how much enforcement effort is applied to the earnings of minors.

Some interest has been manifested in the revival of mandatory joint returns at the state level. In at least one state (Wisconsin) uncertainties of constitutionality have been a considerable factor in discouraging such interest. Although the treatment of family income among countries exhibits many patterns, they may be classified roughly as follows: First there are countries, such as Canada, Australia, and Japan, that apply separate taxation to each spouse. This was the pre-1948 system in the United States. The Canadians, how-

---

[15] Harold M. Groves, *Financing Government* (Henry Holt, 1958), p. 221. "A system which allowed free transfers to spouse and minor children, aggregating gifts to the latter from one donor and spouse to be taxable when the children reached their majority (if in their possession) or thereafter as received, might solve more problems than it creates and would be worth considering." (*Ibid.*, p. 243). (See also Harold M. Groves and Wallace I. Edwards, "A New Model for an Integrated Transfer Tax," *National Tax Journal*, Vol. 6 [December 1953], pp. 353–60.)

ever, have a much stricter law with regard to avoidance devices that constitute in effect the assignment of income between spouses and to children; for instance the income from property gifts to a wife or child is taxed to the husband or parent.

In most of the countries, including all the major countries of Europe, the income of spouses is aggregated, but in most of these, married couples enjoy some mitigation of burden.

This is accomplished by splitting in West Germany, France, and the United States. Only France extends this privilege to cover children, though the latter are conceded only half a split.

Several countries, such as the Netherlands and Sweden, provide for separate rate and/or bracket schedules for married persons with rates on the aggregate income of couples *somewhat* lower than for single persons. The Netherlands extends its rate differentiation to cover size of families in terms of children. Sweden differentiates at the lower end of the scale, but the differences vanish at the top. In addition, it allows a special flat sum deduction if both spouses receive earned income independently and a further allowance of a percentage of a wife's earned income up to a maximum if the couple has a child under sixteen years of age living at home.[16]

Other countries use mandatory joint returns and, with the exception of Great Britain, include the income of minor children in the tax unit. Switzerland excludes *earned* income of children. Other concessions are made, most of them confined to earned income and the dual-income family. Thus in Israel unearned incomes are aggregated, and independently earned incomes are taxed separately under the single rate scale applicable to all individual taxpayers. The British system not only makes general concessions for earned income but adds a special personal allowance and a rate concession to couples if both spouses have earned income. The rate concession, is confined to the first 360 pounds of the earned income of each spouse.

To summarize, treatment in other countries of family income for tax purposes includes: (1) separate taxation of each spouse mainly according to title; (2) splitting; (3) separate rate schedules; (4) mandatory joint returns; and (5) (overlapping other categories) special concessions to the dual-income family confined to earned

---

[16] Oliver Oldman and Ralph Temple, "Comparative Analysis of the Taxation of Married Persons," *Stanford Law Review*, Vol. 12 (May 1960), p. 590.

income and augmented in some cases by an allowance for child care.

The question of the proper unit for taxation was considered at some length by the British Commission on the Taxation of Profits and Income, which reported in 1954.[17] The Commission reported that it had received many suggestions that the aggregation of income of spouses should be abolished. The Commission concluded:[18]

We do not wish to recommend the adoption of either the quotient system (French) or the American system, to which we have alluded above. Each has its attractions, but adoption of either would mean a shift in the distribution of the tax burden from married persons to single ones to an extent that seems to us excessive.

Concerning the allegation that aggregation discourages marriage, the Commission observed that it could give "very little weight to the argument" and added:[19]

First, it is not true as a general statement that aggregation operates as a tax on marriage. It is only true of a man and woman both of whom have incomes and then only if certain ranges of income are exceeded. . . . Secondly, we are skeptical of the suggestion that men and women are in fact dissuaded from marriage by any nice calculation of the financial odds. . . . In the circumstances we think it sufficient to record our view that the reasons that impel men and women to prefer marriage to more casual associations are many and powerful and that the present treatment of married couples for the purpose of tax is not more likely to lead people away from matrimony than to tempt them into it.

Subsequent Legislation

The Revenue Act of 1948 established the principle that a married couple should pay the same tax per person as a single person with one half of the total taxable income. No sooner was the law passed than the Congress began to have doubts that this was entirely fair to single people under all circumstances. Cases were cited of single people with dependents who also share, or partially share, income. After a period of reflection and following an increase in tax

[17] *Second Report*, Her Majesty's Stationery Office (London, 1954), Chapter 6.
[18] *Ibid.*, p. 37.
[19] *Ibid.*, p. 36.

rates in 1951, it appeared that some concessions were required in some cases.

Accordingly, in 1951 Congress established a special category of taxpayers called "heads of households," defined as a single person who maintains a principal place of abode for himself and an unmarried child or grandchild or any other person who is a dependent for tax purposes. In a pragmatic compromise these people were given through a special schedule, a concession which amounts to approximately half the benefit of splitting. It is obvious that the class of single persons like the class of married persons is not homogeneous; but the attempt to open up a special class of single taxpayers for favored treatment was bound to invite enlargement. Thus in 1954 an unsuccessful attempt was made to substitute for the one created in 1951 a class called "heads of families." This category would have been allowed *full* privileges of splitting and would have included single taxpayers with dependents who were close relatives whether or not they lived in the taxpayer's household. However, a new concession was extended to widows and widowers with dependent children; they were allowed a full split, but this privilege was limited to two years after the death of the spouse. The heads-of-household category was expanded to include single persons who support one or more parents in a separate home. Probably most critics would agree that the rationale of all these classificatsons is tenuous.

Analysis of the Issues

The Tax Unit

The first question to consider is that of the proper taxing unit: whether it should be the family unit or the individual (legal owner). Put in equity terms, the question is: Shall two couples with equal taxable incomes pay the same tax regardless of the technical legal division of the income? The consensus of opinion, both lay and expert, seems to be quite predominantly affirmative, and the trend of both statute and court law is in accord.[20] We have no empirical data on the degree to which the income of married couples is in fact

[20] The view that some concessions should be made to working wives is not necessarily an exception. See the discussion below, pp. 80–82, 105.

"pooled," but there is wide agreement on the following points:[21] "First, that spouses in the normal case pool and share their income; second, that the most frequent departures from this practice occur at the upper income levels where there may be a desire to maintain separate fortunes; and third, that pooling and sharing also occur with minor children, but not to the same degree." While pooling in the sense of a common budget may occur less frequently in the top brackets, there are nonetheless benefits in the form of economic power, prestige, and security which are more a function of joint than of separate income.

Beyond this there is the fact that government agencies, as in the administration of public assistance programs, usually consider the family budget as a unit. About one-half of the families in the United States get money income from only one member and are obliged to share for survival. The required support of children is itself a case of sharing. And the quite frequent cases of common bank accounts and joint ownership of property are another instance of the same phenomenon.

There is still support for the view that "the right to a completely separate assessment is an essential part of separate citizenship." But it meets the plausible answer that tax measurement is a matter of ability to pay and economic consequences and in no way curtails the privileges of citizenship, such as the right to vote.

Even though the tax unit be agreed upon, there are still collateral questions to resolve. At least where couples are separated, independent assessment seems appropriate, and the latter might be made optional under conditions where joint returns involve a saving. Then there is the question whether the income of minor children should be included in the aggregate. The earned income of children is frequently regarded as children's spending money outside the family budget. If it were included, there might be a considerable enforcement problem as well as disincentive effects. The latter would be enhanced by the fact that these earnings would be taxed at the taxpayer's marginal rate. More could be said for the Canadian rule of including in the aggregate, investment income of minor children where the property involved comes from the parent.

[21] Douglas Y. Thorson, "The Selection of a Tax Unit Under the Income Tax" (Ph.D. thesis, University of Wisconsin, 1962), p. 189.

The code and court law hardly go beyond defeating transfers that are not *bona fide* or complete.

As already mentioned, the case where both spouses work differs significantly from that where only one is employed. Some adjustments may be in order to recognize this difference. (This problem is discussed below.)

Differentiating the Tax Burden: The Split-Income Plan

Once the question of a proper unit is settled, the major remaining issue is that of differentiating tax burdens according to size of family. This is partly a matter of exemptions but leaving this (and the matter of sharing with children) aside, the question may be stated: What relative taxes should married couples and single persons with the same taxable income pay? Does splitting give us an acceptable answer?

NUMBERS OF BENEFICIARIES. We may begin this exercise with an account of who got and who gets the benefit of splitting and what these benefits are worth. First, it should be noted that no benefit accrues to those couples whose joint returns have taxable income under $2,000 and that the value of the benefit for those in the $2,000–$4,000 income classes rises from $0 to $40 within that range. The $40 difference in the case of a $4,000 income is a reduction of about 5 percent below the tax on a single person with the same income and number of exemptions. Based on 1960 figures, 63 percent of the joint returns with taxable income benefit from splitting to the extent of $40 or less.

Above the $4,000 taxable-income level the savings begin to mount rapidly. The effective tax for a married couple is about 29 percent below that for a single person with the same income and exemptions at $24,000. Thereafter the percentage of difference decreases, but the absolute difference keeps on mounting up to incomes of $400,000, where the benefit stands at $25,180. The difference begins to disappear at slightly over $600,000, where single persons are at their maximum average rate of 87 percent. Married persons continue to pay at a marginal rate of 91 percent until their income reaches $1,200,000, at which level no further benefit of splitting is possible. (See Table 3.)

TABLE 3. Federal Tax Liabilities of Married Persons and Single Persons with Equal Incomes Under Split-Income Plan Limited to Spouses
(1954–63)

Taxable Income	Tax differential	Differential as a percentage of single person's tax
$ 2,000	$ 0	0.0%
4,000	40	4.8
6,000	120	8.8
8,000	280	14.3
10,000	440	16.7
12,000	680	20.0
14,000	940	22.1
16,000	1,280	24.7
18,000	1,600	25.8
20,000	1,980	27.3
22,000	2,340	27.9
26,000	3,080	28.7
32,000	4,060	28.1
38,000	4,900	26.7
44,000	5,740	25.6
50,000	6,520	24.3
60,000	7,880	23.0
70,000	9,300	22.1
80,000	10,740	21.4
90,000	12,180	20.8
100,000	13,680	20.3
150,000	19,480	17.4
200,000	22,180	14.1
400,000	25,180	7.4
600,000	25,180	4.8
1,000,000	10,360	1.2
1,300,000	0	0.0

Source: Douglas Y. Thorson, *op. cit.,* Appendix B, Table V, adapted.

Of course, single taxpayers gain nothing unless they fall under one of the special categories created by legislation subsequent to the 1948 law. Couples where spouses have equal independent incomes gain nothing; the tax savings increase with the degree of income inequality between the spouses. As compared with mandatory joint returns, married couples with only one income enjoy the full benefit of splitting.

A special calculation made by Douglas Thorson for the author concludes that as of 1958, 66.5 percent of all returns either did not qualify for the benefits of splitting to begin with, or else derived little or no benefits because their incomes were too low. Only about 17 percent of all returns received significantly more than $40 in benefits—those with an adjusted gross income above $7,000.[22]

Many people think of any "reform" of the present income-splitting plan in terms of imposing additional burdens on *married* taxpayers. This ignores the fact that the problem is one of relative burdens. It can be conceived rather in terms of relief for *single* taxpayers. If the single taxpayers were to be granted the privilege of splitting with themselves, so to speak, the major problem remaining would be that of a proper graduation of the rate scale. And the number of single taxpayers involved in the change and the loss of revenue would be far less than occurred in 1948. For instance, our calculations show that to give all single taxpayers the present status of householders (half a split) would reduce total revenue by only $650 million.

Commenting on a proposal that single persons be given the privilege of splitting their incomes generally, Pechman analyzed the problem as follows:[23]

Finally, if all single persons with dependents were granted the tax advantages of income splitting, one might well question whether there would be any point in retaining the remaining vestiges of the old distinction between single persons and married couples. As Table 4 shows, in 1956 out of a total of 19.6 million tax returns with adjusted gross income above $5,000 (where the tax advantages of income splitting began to have some significance), 17.8 million were returns of married couples. Of the remaining 1.8 million, 317,000 were heads of households and 38,000 were persons whose spouses had died in one of the two preceding years. Another 409,000 single people had one or more dependents. If this group

---

[22] Other calculations may be cited. Roy Blough: "Only about 22 percent of married couples were estimated to receive sufficient income in 1948 to have their taxes reduced by income splitting." (*The Federal Taxing Process* [Prentice-Hall, 1952], pp. 320–21.) Daniel M. Holland and C. Harry Kahn: "In all, the returns that benefited from income splitting constituted less than 29 percent of all (separate and joint) taxable returns in 1951, but received 59 percent of taxable income ("Comparison of Personal and Taxable Income," *Federal Tax Policy for Economic Growth and Stability*, U. S. Congress, Joint Committee on the Economic Report [Washington, 1956], pp. 313–38).

[23] Joseph A. Pechman, "Income Splitting," testimony submitted to the House Committee on Ways and Means, *Tax Revision Compendium*, Vol. 1 (November 1959), p. 484.

were given the privilege of income splitting, there would remain only a million single persons with incomes above $5,000, or a little more than 5 percent of all taxpayer units above that level, who would continue to be taxed at the very steep rates now in the law.

LOSS OF REVENUE AND EFFECT ON PROGRESSIVITY. Obviously the effect on progression of splitting was to reduce it quite drastically for some taxpayers in some ranges and substantially in terms of the over-all pattern of effective rates on family incomes by income classes. For the couple with dependents, very little progression in marginal rates will occur below the $8,000-level of taxable income ($10,200 adjusted gross income). Average rates for the gainers were reduced 1.0 point at $4,000 and 13.7 points at $100,000 taxable income.

As to loss of revenue, one of the best available recent figures appears to be that of Pechman.[24] Using 1956 data, he calculated that the difference in yield under income splitting and under his own proposal of narrowing the brackets for married couples would be $3.8 billion. Our own calculation, based on 1959 data, indicates a figure of $4.3 billion. Using 1951 data, Holland and Kahn calculated that the elimination of splitting would finance a $100 increase in per capita exemptions, or an upper limit of 50 percent on marginal rates, or a reduction of all rates by 2.5 percentage points.[25]

However, it may be argued plausibly that very large revenues depend not on income-splitting as such, but rather on the level and degree of graduation of tax rates that Congress finds acceptable. In this view it is unrealistic to measure the opportunity costs of income-splitting by the standard of rates applying to single persons. Possible changes in the law should be viewed as concessions to single taxpayers rather than as imposing higher burdens for married couples.[26]

Here it should be added that none of the above proves that income-splitting is inequitable or inexpedient. There is nothing sacred about the pre-1948 standard or any other standard. These standards still need to be compared in terms of equity and/or of socio-economic effects. The above analysis indicates that it is doubtful that

[24] *Ibid.*, p. 478.
[25] *Op. cit.*, p. 334.
[26] Comment by Lawrence H. Seltzer on an earlier draft of this paper.

Congress or the public ever intended to alter the distribution of the tax burden in the way that ex-post analysis shows that it did.

PHILOSOPHY. Two distinct approaches to the philosophy of equity in taxation were presented in Chapter I. The classical theory of equal sacrifice could probably be enlisted to support some pattern of splitting. The utility of foregone consumption (sacrifice) is directly related to numbers. Two people have greater capacity for sacrifice than one. Common sense tells us that a couple could hardly each live as well—be as "well off"—as a single person with the same income. (Here we may ignore the fact that budget studies indicate that a married couple can maintain the same standard as a single person on less than twice the latter's income.) The couple has some advantage in terms of security since the capacity of either to earn assures at least some income for the unit. But this is perhaps a minor consideration. It should be noted, however, that the logic of the per capita approach requires not only division between spouses but also with children—at least in some degree. And probably few proponents of splitting would be prepared to accept this ultimate solution as the French have done. The logic would also dictate differentiation over the entire range of income—not merely in the middle ranges. Either a multiple rate scale or a per capita personal exemption expressed as a constant percentage of income would probably better suit the logic of equal sacrifice.

The socio-economic approach might give a different answer. Here, as previously noted, the principal concern in the case of those at the bottom of the income scale is for the maintenance of human resources, and this would appear to be a per capita matter. But this area of concern is principally with families having incomes below $10,000, where splitting, under the present model at least, has very little effect. At the top of the scale, the concern is with the concentration of power (in one or all of several senses), and this is usually a family, and not a personal, matter. The purpose of progression in the middle range is something of a hiatus in this doctrine. Progression here can perhaps be viewed as the connecting link to preserve a smooth scale, which in general seeks to check extremes in the distribution of power. The concern for human resources at the lower income levels can be expressed in the exemption system.

Like the degree of progression, if any, the choice between these two philosophies must rest in considerable degree on personal preference. All that the scholar can do is to clarify the analysis (and assemble any available factual evidence) upon which such preference should be based.

MARRIAGE. But there are other interests to consider. The one most emphasized in popular discussion is the effect on marriage of aggregating income without splitting. It is true that the consensus of expert and other disinterested opinion[27] has been highly skeptical of the allegation that the morals of the nation and the propensity to get married and stay married are critically at stake in any solution of the family tax problem. But the matter probably should not be dismissed as mere "feminist sentiment." Other things being equal, we would at least prefer a system that does not associate higher taxes with marriage. It should be noted that under any system proposed there is no penalty on marriage unless the spouses have, and will continue to have, two independent incomes. Marriage under splitting (as compared with the pre-1948 situation) gives a positive tax advantage only to those with unequal independent incomes. The same is generally true for taxpayers in the very high and the lowest brackets.

INCENTIVE. Splitting affects incentives in various ways. For one thing it avoids discouraging married women from taking or keeping jobs. Critics will differ on whether the recent influx of married women into the labor force is desirable or not, but most would agree that, other things being equal, they would prefer a tax system which is neutral on the matter. Neutrality here, of course, is a matter of degree; the wife's earnings will be taxed in any event but with lesser penalty from marginal rates under splitting. The claims of the two-job couple for special consideration will be considered later in this chapter.

It has been alleged that the special concession to the middle brackets involved in splitting supports the presently weak incentives

[27] Thorson sent questionnaires to 25 randomly selected Madison clergymen on this matter. Of the 22 who replied, all answered that potentially higher rates of tax following marriage would have no effect on the institution of matrimony. (Douglas Y. Thorson, op. cit., p. 218n.)

for advancement for business executives. In reply it is argued that the splitting device is ill-conceived for this purpose since it does nothing for the executive who is single. Moreover, eliminating splitting would conserve enough revenue to reduce at least the nominal marginal rates for all taxpayers; and if confined to the brackets where splitting is important, the reduction would be quite substantial.

Analysis of Other Proposals

Some of the pros and cons of alternative proposals remain to be considered. Little need be said about a return to the old federal system of optional joint and separate returns. This would bring with it all of the problems that impelled action in 1948. The mandatory-joint-return proposal has a respectable following, but it ranks very low in political feasibility. Chairman Millikin of the Senate Finance Committee, commenting on the mandatory-joint-return proposal of a witness, observed in 1948:[28] "I may refresh your memory: we tried it several times. The only . . . (difficulty) with it is that you cannot get the votes to make a law of it."

Proposals for a dual schedule or bracket system *might* fare better politically, and they have other advantages that are substantial.

The dual-rate-scale plan is an especially flexible instrument, and it permits an almost infinite number of compromises. Married couples could be given *some* advantage over single taxpayers with the same taxable income but less than our present law allows. This is the practice apparently in several European countries. Taking a leaf from the Swedish practice, the plan might confine the married-taxpayer concession to the lower brackets. This would make a great deal of sense in terms of the socio-economic approach to progressive taxation. Going Sweden one better, one could confine the concession to families where both spouses are employed, though this would precipitate considerable difficulty in defining what constitutes employment.

Dual rate scales could be adjusted easily to extend a concession to married couples within the first bracket of income. Possibly a

---

[28] U. S. Senate, Committee on Finance, *Reduction of Individual Income Taxes*, Hearings on H.R. 4970, 80 Cong. 2 sess. (1948), p. 272.

single person with a $2,000 *taxable* income should pay more taxes than a couple with the same taxable income. However, personal exemption policy is especially important at the lowest bracket level, and it already allows a married couple considerable advantage. Under our federal system a married couple with a $2,000 (adjusted gross) income pays one-half as much tax as a single person with the same income. And this is without benefit of splitting.

Dual rate schedules would complicate the statute and the tax return, but this could hardly be serious and certainly no worse than the present dual rate schedule for heads of households.

The Pechman split-bracket plan is simpler than dual rate schedules, and it has several other important advantages, at least over mandatory joint returns. It would have much the same effect in terms of distribution as mandatory joint returns, but by allowing universal splitting between spouses, it would involve no conflict between the community property and the common law states. By allowing a choice between joint and separate returns, but with the advantage generally with the former, it would automatically provide for cases of spouses who wish to be treated as single and who can so elect though they would still bear the higher rate of the married status.

Pechman noted that the effect of the 1948 legislation was to double the width of the brackets for married couples, and he proposed to undo this by a rate schedule with brackets half as wide for married taxpayers as for single taxpayers. In support of this he argued that the acquisition of a spouse by a single person would justify granting him an additional exemption but no further rebate merely because he prefers to spend part of his income on a wife "rather than to spend it in other ways."[29] He gave considerable weight to the view that the distinctions of the present law, both between married and unmarried taxpayers and between some single taxpayers and others, are tenuous and noted that the present system has undesirable and unwanted effects on progression and the revenue.

The Vickrey proposal, on the other hand, aims at per capita taxation without sacrifice in progression or revenue. It would do nothing to please those who object to the present system on the

[29] Pechman, *op. cit.*, p. 479.

score that it favors (some) married couples over their single counter-parts. Its principal advantage is that it does not impose higher taxes when two persons with independent incomes marry. By the same token this is a principal objection to the Pechman plan. On the other hand, the Vickrey plan gives what its critics regard as an unwarrant-ed boon to the married couple with one income.

Vickrey's proposal, presented prior to the 1948 legislation, would leave the assessment of joint returns as at that time (1947) "but single and separate returns would be required to use a surtax scale in which the brackets . . . are half those now in effect,"[30] thus substantially augmenting the tax on single taxpayers. Of course, the level of rates is adjustable in order to raise whatever revenue is desired. In addition to the effects of marriage, Vickrey rests his case for this proposal on ability to pay in terms of sacrifice; on the fact that sharing of income in some sense involves a redistribution; and on the proposition that there is no reason why two persons should pay a higher tax "because they happen to live together in a single household."[31] He also proposed an earned income credit that would give further relief to the two-job family.

Concessions to Householders

As previously mentioned, householders as defined under the U. S. tax law are allowed a concession that amounts to half the ad-vantage of splitting, and widows and widowers with dependent children enjoy full benefit of splitting for two years after the death of their spouses.

Both theoretical and practical objections may be offered to these makeshifts. If dependents, at least adult dependents, are to be accepted as members of the taxpaying unit, it is hard to see why they should not qualify as such whether or not the taxpayer is married and regardless of where they live, which seems irrelevant. Moreover, the provision which allows the taxpayer the concession in some cases, even though the member of the household is not a dependent and has an independent non-aggregated income making him a taxpayer in his own right, is hardly defensible. Were it granted that householders should pay less taxes than other single

[30] Vickrey, *op. cit.*, p. 285.
[31] *Ibid.*, p. 280.

people, objection could still be made that the present concession, as was pointed out above, benefits only a small portion of householders. The extension of splitting to some single people and not to others is essentially arbitrary.

Working Wives

The point can be made and supported that there is at least as much reason for giving a higher concession to the two-job family (marital unit) than to the one-job family as there is for a higher concession to the one-job family than to a single person. This is not a matter of independent title to income, though as indicated above, the two-job family with spouses earning equal incomes gains nothing from splitting (as compared with the pre-1948 situation) and is the one that would marry into higher brackets under a mandatory-joint-return plan or its equivalent. The claim for concession rests first on the extra expense associated with two jobs. The working wife incurs the expense of transportation to and from her work, the extra clothes required for her job, and the extra cost of preparing food for the household. Here again the class is not homogeneous, and still greater expense may be involved if the working wife has small children and no built-in baby sitters such as grandparents. Some attempt has been made in the law to recognize this special situation with a deduction for the cost of child care. It may be noted that it is a heavily hedged provision thought by many critics to be niggardly.

Another approach would emphasize the untaxed imputed income of the wife who spends her time in the household.

In addition to all this, if taxable family income is equal, the worker in the one-job family has the more lucrative job carrying the greater prestige and permitting one spouse to enjoy more leisure. The one-job family also enjoys greater security perhaps since the nonemployed spouse is in reserve to earn the family income if the present breadwinner should become incapacitated. The working wife is also in reserve in some sense, but it is reasonable to assume that under the condition of equal family income the nonworking wife will often have earning power greater than that of the working wife.

Neither the extra expense of the working wife nor the imputed income of the nonworking wife can be measured with any acceptable degree of precision. It is probably true that the additional expenses of the working wife rise with her earnings and that in some degree the imputed value of the services of the nonworking wife are related to the size of her husband's income. As to such special expenses as the cost of transportation and work clothes, the rise is probably less than proportional to that of earnings. In any event the higher outlay that is associated with a more remunerative position involves a greater degree of personal choice and discretion.

It should be noted that there is more justification for a concession under mandatory joint returns than under the split-income provision; the latter already favors married couples, and additional relief would shift still greater relative burden to single people.

If it were concluded that the two-job family deserves a special concession, there are several forms that it might take. A double exemption has the merit of simplicity, but it takes no account of the fact that expenses and the value of imputed services increase as income rises. Thorson favors a special deduction proportional to the wife's income but "with a specific upper limit and restricted to low and modest incomes."[32] A special rate scale like that used in Sweden, with concessions confined to the two-job family and decreasing as income mounts, can also be commended for attention.[33]

Child-Care

As previously suggested, the present provision for child-care expense introduced in 1954, is tightly circumscribed, and it may be classified as an attempt to relieve extreme hardship cases. Employed women and widowers are allowed to deduct up to $600 for expenses

[32] *Op. cit.*, p. 243.

[33] In either case there are some difficulties in defining "employment." Our present child-care expense deduction is limited to expenses incurred (and $600), and the expenses must be incurred to enable the taxpayer to be gainfully employed in or outside the home. The taxpayer may or may not be self-employed. The British have long allowed concessions to so-called earned income, including, within strict limits, the income of a self-employment business. Both experiences give some clue to our problem of defining a two-job family. Probably the definition would have to be couched in terms of time spent by the second job-holding spouse in remunerative work whether within or without the household.

paid during the tax year for the care of dependent children under 12 and other dependents incapable of caring for themselves. Employment may be within or without the home, and the taxpayer may or may not be self-employed. The concession is for all dependents and may not be augmented where more than one person is involved in the care. In the case of married women (except where the husband is physically or mentally incapable of support) the amount otherwise allowable must be reduced by any excess of their adjusted gross income over $4,500.

We have noted earlier that a persuasive case can be made for further concessions to working wives, but granting this, the question remains as to whether the distinction among working wives recognized by the present statute should be preserved and perhaps broadened. While child-care allowances presently have a fairly limited application,[34] there appears to be ample ground for maintaining a provision of this kind for special cases. The present ceiling on joint earnings seems unduly restrictive and might well be doubled.

Summary and Conclusion

Recapitulating several important points in our discussion of income splitting, we note that:

1. Our present problem and institutions are the product of legal, historical, and political factors; the law of 1948 eliminated territorial inequality, but it is highly doubtful that the narrow and capricious pattern of benefits it dispensed was ever intended to correct previous inequalities in the distribution of the tax load among families.

2. A strong consensus supports the view that the proper taxing unit is the family unit; that is, that two couples with equal taxable income should pay the same regardless of the technical legal division of the income.

3. Proponents of splitting can claim some sanction in the classical theory of equal sacrifice; the socio-economic philosophy, stress-

---

[34] In 1960, 272,000 child-care exemptions were claimed on all returns, 244,000 on taxable returns. The dollar value of these two figures was $103 million and $92 million, respectively. In 1960 alimony payments claimed as an itemized deduction totaled $219 million.

ing power, supports graduation by family units without regard to the number in the family group.

4. Recognition that the 1948 law was unfair to some single people has taken the form of extending the benefits of splitting to them in some cases. The classifications established, however, fall short of rational defensibility. The experience lends support to the view that the entire class of single taxpayers is entitled to (relative) tax relief.

5. Of suggested reforms, dual rate schedules (including the manipulation of bracket widths) have most to commend them. They could be designed to close the gap in relative tax burdens as between single persons and married couples either in whole or in part without reviving the old issues between community property and common law states.

6. A strong case can be made in terms largely of extra expense incurred by working wives and the nontaxability of the imputed value of services of nonworking wives, for granting some concessions to the two-job family. This might take the form of a special deduction proportional to the wife's earnings, with a specified upper limit and restricted to low and modest incomes.

7. A deduction for working wives would mitigate the problem of penalizing marriage implicit in any plan of progression which ignores family size. Other things being equal, a tax system neutral as to matrimony is preferred; but there is little evidence to support the view that this interest alone should be allowed to order the tax system.

8. A strong case can also be made for more generous allowance for child-care than that now granted. The family that must incur out-of-pocket expense in order to keep both spouses working is entitled to treat some part of what seems to be net income as in fact gross income.

9. Very large revenues are at stake in the issue of splitting. Few other structural provisions in the law are equivalent to an average of 2.5 percentage points in the marginal rates.

CHAPTER V

Effect of Changes in the Law on Tax Rates

FURTHER CALCULATIONS OF THE quantitative importance of some of the possible changes (considered individually and in packages) discussed in the previous chapters are presented here. As previously indicated, the issue in income splitting is mainly one of relative burdens, particularly as between married couples and single taxpayers. Relative burdens may be considered in either of two contexts: (1) of expanded revenue, with the statutory rate scale remaining constant and the changes in effective rates both adding to revenue and changing the relative position of different taxpayers; or (2) of constant revenue, with positive changes in effective rates for some taxpayers being used to reduce the over-all rate scale and thus give a positive benefit to other taxpayers.

Chart 3 shows absolute and relative burdens under present law.[1] Especially noteworthy is the wide gap between the two lines representing effective rates for married couples and single taxpayers. Moreover, the chart shows that with full splitting, the gap in effective rates for the two groups of taxpayers continues to diverge within the $0 to $50,000 income range. Beyond $28,000, however,

[1] The charts and estimates in this chapter are largely the work of Mr. Edward Wiegner, who assisted the author in the preparation of this manuscript.

CHART 3. Effective Rates of Tax for Different Family Statuses Under Present Provisions

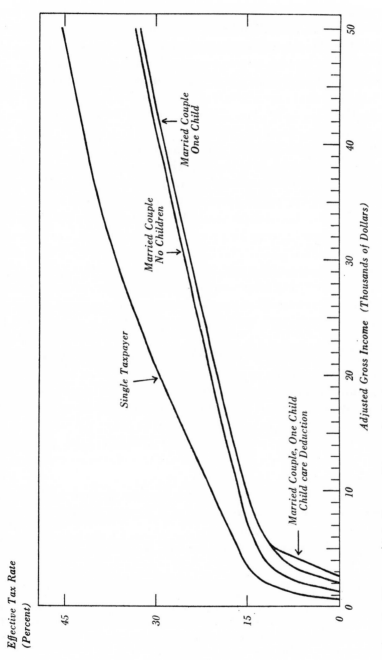

*Effective Tax Rate
(Percent)*

Single Taxpayer

Married Couple
No Children

Married Couple
One Child

Married Couple, One Child
Child care Deduction

Adjusted Gross Income (Thousands of Dollars)

Assuming 10 percent deductions at all income levels.

the difference in rates between the two groups relative to their total burdens begins to decline.[2] The dotted lines indicate the reduction in burden for married taxpayers with children in case they qualify for the present child-care allowance. If expenditures equal or exceed the limit, and if the couple has adjusted gross income of $4,500 or less, the child-care deduction is the equivalent of another $600 exemption. Its value then diminishes dollar for dollar in terms of base as income exceeds $4,500.

Chart 4 shows absolute and relative burdens that would exist were present provisions of the law with regard to splitting modified in various ways and no changes made in statutory rates. Since all of the changes favor added revenue, the chart indicates some reduction in relative burdens for some classes of taxpayers but no reduction in absolute burdens for anyone. Thus the changes are those that might be contemplated were more revenue needed. The changes selected for presentation are: (1) to provide no splitting at all either by mandatory joint returns or by the split-bracket procedure, as in the Pechman plan; (2) to provide a half split for married couples in lieu of, and following the same model as, that now provided for single "heads of households." (As previously noted, the half-split might be accepted as a "pragmatic compromise" by proponents of different philosophies or as a means of reducing what seems to many as an unwarranted discrimination against single taxpayers.) Introduced also in the chart is a deduction for working wives.[3]

It will be noted that under the no-split plans, effective rates for single taxpayers and married couples follow each other closely, the difference between them being due to the additional exemption for married taxpayers. The half-split shows the compromise character of its origin: the divergence between burdens of single and married taxpayers follows the same pattern as in the case of full splitting, but it is much less pronounced.

The allowance for working wives in the case of the two-job

[2] All figures here and in subsequent charts are computed on the assumption that deductions equal 10 percent of gross income.

[3] Here we assumed a deduction based on 10 percent of the spouse's income up to $5,000, after which the base would be reduced dollar for dollar by the excess. The spouse's income was assumed to be 40 percent of joint income. On these terms its maximum value of $500 occurs at $12,500 of joint income, and it vanishes at $25,000.

CHART 4. Effective Rates of Tax for Different Family Statuses and Income-Splitting Provisions

Gain in Revenue Redounding to the Treasury

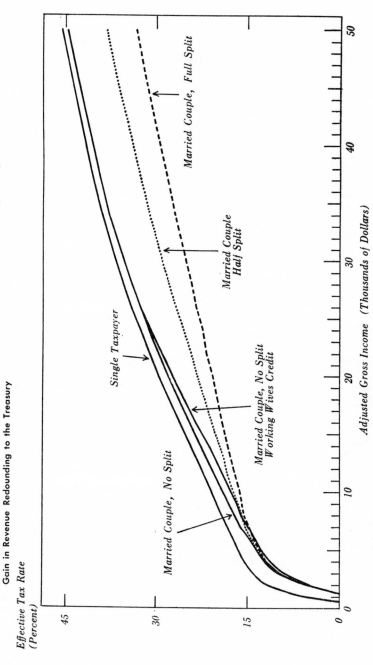

Effective Tax Rate
(Percent)

45

30

15

0

Single Taxpayer

Married Couple, No Split

Married Couple, No Split
Working Wives Credit

Married Couple
Half Split

Married Couple, Full Split

0   10   20   30   40   50

Adjusted Gross Income   (Thousands of Dollars)

Assuming 10 percent deductions at all income levels, and present rates.

TABLE 4. Revenue Gains and Losses from Various Changes in the Individual Income Tax at 1959 Income Levels

Tax Changes	Revenue Gain (+) or Loss (−)*
Elimination of the 10% standard deduction and limitation of itemized deductions to those in excess of 10% of adjusted gross income	$+7,238,500,000[a]
Elimination of the second exemption for the aged and the blind	+ 425,500,000[b]
Substitution of a $120 tax credit for the present $600 continuing exemption	+1,238,000,000[c]
Elimination of the Retirement Income Credit	+ 111,000,000[d]
Elimination of Splitting	+4,275,000,000[e]
Allowing Social Security contributions by employee and self-employed as deductions and including benefit payments in adjusted gross income	− 432,000,000[f,g]
Net Gains of Total Package	$ 12,856,000,000

* Gains are based on 1959 returns and are for proposals when considered as a package.

[a] For taxable returns, 10% of adjusted gross income was added to taxable income where either standard or itemized deductions were taken.

The base gain of $25,938 million was added to the present base, and the total taxable income by income classes was distributed to the estimated appropriate income tax brackets. The yield was then recomputed on the new base, and subtracting the old yield from the new gave the amount of tax gain.

The estimate does not include any revenue gain from nontaxable returns although there clearly would be some. The value of exemptions exceeds adjusted gross income in most income classes, and this makes it very difficult to make any reliable estimate of gain, which undoubtedly would be small. The estimate thus errs on the conservative side.

[b] The base gain on taxable returns of $1,978,825,000 was distributed into the estimated appropriate tax brackets, and the appropriate marginal rates were applied to give an estimate of increased yield. (The methodology is like that used in note a above.)

For the same reason as above, the estimate does not include any gains from nontaxable returns and thus errs considerably on the conservative side.

[c] The estimated gain from introduction of a tax credit is based on a subtraction of the cost of credits from the cost of the present continuing exemptions. Present exemption cost was determined by adding exemptions back into taxable income in each income class and subtracting the present yield from the yield with the exemptions added into taxable income.

[d] The gain from the elimination of the retirement income credit is the full value of the credits on taxable and nontaxable returns. Credits on nontaxable returns are included because analysis of the returns indicates that all claimed credits are actually used to offset income taxes.

[e] The estimate of gain from the elimination of splitting is based on a reallocation of taxable income into the brackets and rates used for returns of single taxpayers. Reduction of the split to half its present value rather than complete elimination would regain $2,110 million on joint returns.

[f] All the social security changes should be viewed as only very rough approximations. For example, distributions of social security payments within each money income class were not available, so the total distribution of social security payments was assumed independent of the distribution of money income. This certainly is not valid because social security payments are a part of total money income, and as social security payments rise, so does money income. In spite of these and other limitations, however, the figures can be used to give some rough idea of the magnitudes involved.

In 1959 total contributions to OASDI by employees and the self-employed was $4,732 million. A reduction of 8.5% was made in this amount for contributions on nontaxable returns, but due to a lack of information no reduction was made for contributions by non-reporting individuals. The resulting effective deductions were valued at a marginal rate of 22.83%, which was derived as the mean marginal rate on all returns.

family is shown on the chart as it might be under a no-split arrangement. Of course, the concession in this case would apply to a much smaller class than married couples generally.

Chart 5 examines relative incidence in a context where revenue is held constant and the savings from changes are used to reduce rates generally. There are various ways in which rate schedules can be reduced so as to hold total revenue constant: In our illustrations we have chosen a proportionate reduction in all rates for both the partial and the complete elimination of splitting. Thus if a specific change would increase revenues from $30 to $40 billion, the present 20–91 percent rates would be cut to $15-68\frac{1}{4}$ percent to bring revenues back to $30 billion.

As expected, the chart indicates that the more splitting allowed, the higher the resulting rates for single taxpayers. Also as expected, the more splitting allowed, the lower the rates for married taxpayers in the range above $8,000–$8,500 adjusted gross income. However, below this level, the incidence is surprising and striking. The no-split pattern provides the *lowest* rates for married couples, while the half-split pattern produces a somewhat higher effective burden and the full-split one the highest of all. This paradoxical result is explained by the fact that in the lower ranges of income, splitting provides no, or negligible, advantage, and the rate of relief available from the elimination of splitting more than compensates for loss of this advantage. The generalization that nearly everyone would

---

As to the taxability of benefits, the analysis was divided into two parts: (1) tax gains from those individuals who were receiving only social security payments, and (2) tax gains from those individuals who had money income in addition to social security.

For beneficiaries receiving only social security payments a distribution of recipients by size of monthly grant was used to distribute total payments to each size of benefit. Then for each benefit size the portion of the benefit taxable to one- and two-dependent families was determined to estimate how much of the payments to that benefit size were taxable. The addition of gains in all sizes yielded $900 million of taxable income, to which a rate of 20% was applied.

For recipients who were receiving other additional money income a distribution of social security payments by money income classes was derived. By viewing social security payments as additional to already taxable income and allowing exemptions for one- and two-dependent families, it was again possible to make some calculation of the gain in tax base for each money income class. The total gains were $1,825 million of base, to which a marginal rate of 20.6% was applied. The rate exceeds 20% to account for those individuals with money income who were already in the over 20% brackets.

Principal information sources for these calculations are "Money Income of Aged Persons, A 10-Year Review, 1948–1958," *Social Security Bulletin*, Vol. 22 (June 1959) and "Money Income of Aged Persons, Mid-1960," *Social Security Bulletin*, Vol. 24 (January 1961), by Lenore A. Epstein; and the "Annual Statistical Supplement, 1959."

[g] An alternative plan for treating social security receipts would be to disallow any deduction for contributions and to tax that portion of receipts which were not previously contributed by the beneficiary. This would replace the loss indicated in the table with a positive figure of $540 million and would add approximately a billion dollars to the net gain of the total package.

CHART 5. Effective Rates of Tax for Different Statuses and Income-Splitting Provisions
Revenue Gains Used to Reduce All Rates Proportionately

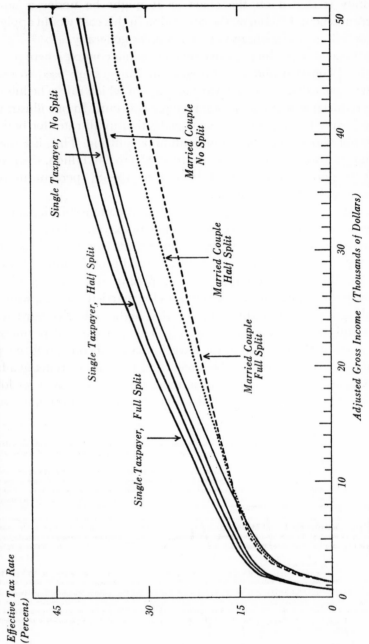

Assuming 10 percent deductions at all income levels, and present or proportionately reduced rates for half- or no-splitting.

gain from the elimination of splitting finds some support in this chart.[4]

Next we have made certain rough estimates of the tax savings that would result from some of the major changes considered in this manuscript, the savings being translated into rate reductions. Again we have selected a proportional reduction in rates for illustrative purposes though it is only one among several possible rate reduction patterns. The present scale of tax rates for a single taxpayer starts at 20 percent on the first $2,000 of taxable income, rises to 50 percent on taxable income in excess of $18,000, and to 91 percent on taxable income in excess of $200,000. Tax savings of the magnitude shown in Table 4 would finance a proportionate reduction in taxes (exclusive of capital gains) of $25\frac{1}{4}$ percent. Thus rates of 20 percent, 50 percent, and 91 percent would be reduced to approximately 15 percent, $37\frac{1}{2}$ percent, and 68 percent.

It will be noted that a revenue loss rather than gain is calculated for the modification in treatment of social security (full taxation of benefits and current deduction of the contributions of employees and the self-employed). Accordingly, this change must seek justification in terms of equity, on which basis an adequate defense can be made for it. The loss, of course, is due to the transfer of taxable income over time from a period (in the life of the taxpayer) of high income to one of lower income.

If the theoretically correct procedure of allowing a deduction only for that portion of receipts previously contributed by the beneficiary were followed, the substantial loss could be converted into an equally substantial gain.

It will be noted that only a few of the changes considered above would plug what the critics have commonly criticized as "loopholes." Therefore, they do not exhaust the possibilities of "broadening the tax base" though they might make other means of doing so more palatable.

In conclusion, it should be noted again that if income tax revenues are to be maintained, it will not be possible to reduce *effective* rates for every taxpayer except by including persons now excluded by personal exemptions and deductions. Nor will it be pos-

[4] Because of the difficulty in calculating with any precision the revenue effects of an allowance for working wives, this modification is omitted from this chart.

sible, while maintaining the present degree of progression, to reduce effective marginal rates. Accordingly, gains for incentives and/or equity must come mainly from: (1) the redistribution of the tax load; and (2) the reduction in the gap between stated rates and effective rates. But this is also true of other means of broadening the tax base.

CHAPTER VI

Summary of Conference Discussion

A TWO-DAY CONFERENCE on the tax treatment of the family proved a first-rate exercise in normative economics. Reasonable and well-informed men may differ on nearly all the important issues in this area, and they did so at this conference. Some critics find such exercises of dubious value noting that on matters of this sort "one opinion is as good as another."[1] Nevertheless, it is the author's impression that the conference was highly successful both in defining and sharpening issues and in laying bare the underpinnings on which sharp differences are based. It also supplied the author with several new ideas that he had neglected in the preparation of the background paper. These notes on the conference attempt to provide both a summary of the meeting and some of the author's thoughts stimulated by the experience. No votes were taken to indicate consensus, and any generalizations in this regard are the author's impressions and should be discounted for his own biases.

[1] One participant said, "It seems to me that the trouble with this approach—and there is no criticism of this particular manuscript, but it is just in the nature of the topic—you immediately jump in and mix up norms without any sort of positive analysis. What is needed in this area just as in all these areas if we are to make any progress at all is to try to get our positive analysis worked out first before we start talking about what should be." Another said:

"I don't think that 27 economists should have been assembled to address themselves to problems which are really partly anthropological, partly sociological, partly anything except what we have competence in."

It soon became apparent that the members of the conference would divide fairly sharply into two schools of thought. One school regards a per capita approach to family taxation, at least when applied to adults, as the only one that makes sense in judging taxpayers' capacities at the horizontal level, and also the best index for judging vertical differences. The idea that family status itself, outside of the numbers involved, can affect comparisons is repugnant to them and is a case of regarding spouses (no children) as an article of consumption rather than as people. Each person should count for one and only one. Marriage is analogous to a partnership in which the partners have an equal stake; and the partnership as such neither adds to nor subtracts from taxpaying capacity.[2] Some went so far as to say that even if the partnership did enhance economic welfare, the choice of a more (or less) efficient way of utilizing income should have no bearing on tax burdens. On the other hand, marriage usually involves a genuine redistribution of income, which the tax laws should recognize.

The other group holds that family status and the circumstances of family living are relevant factors in gauging tax capacity. Thus two married persons with the same per capita income as a single person may have more taxpaying capacity than the latter. This could be, so it is alleged, because a married couple, other things being equal, can "live better" or enjoy a higher economic scale of living than can the single person with the same per capita income.[3] Moreover, two married people only one of whom contributes di-

[2] As two members of the Conference said, "In any event (when) people are married, they should be looked upon as being in a partnership. When people get divorced, this is a change. If you had a partnership, and you had a split-off of a partner, and in the course of this the total income fell, I think it would be proper to observe the fact and to tax accordingly. I don't see any difficulty on this score at all."

"Whether people live together in groups or whether they don't depends upon tastes and depends on costs, and I should think a first principle is that the government has no interest in this kind of question. That's their business whether they choose to live one way or another. So can't we just eliminate that as irrelevant here. If you are going to treat it as relevant, then you have to say that people who live in boarding houses should be taxed more than people who live in apartment houses."

[3] "I would like the record to show that I don't feel any poorer by virtue of the fact that I am married." Another participant said:

"Do you think that (Mr. X) was a different man the day after his divorce than before for tax purposes? Should we make a differentiation of $28,000 in his tax liability, to be exact? Incidentally his tax liability rose if he had the same income."

rectly to the aggregate income may be "better off" than two people who both contribute. This could be so because, for instance, the working wife is obliged to incur extra expense associated either with her job, or her home, or both, and there is a probability that she will contribute less non-money income to the family than she would if she were not working. The sense in which this view regards people as articles of consumption is not cannibalistic; it only relates family groupings to relevant tests of welfare. Redistribution of income within the family circle has no significance apart from such tests. All of this is aside from the social consideration of power distribution that is stressed in the background paper.[4]

The difference indicated above may or may not go deeper than the criteria to be used in applying the income tax to the family. Perhaps they go to the nature and behavior of the family itself.

Criteria

This account of opposing views is presented largely in terms of comparative welfare, and this criterion for gauging tax capacity kept reappearing throughout the conference. The approach has some sanction in classical doctrine of equal sacrifice or opportunity cost; it also is in line with the social goal of impinging as little as possible upon the socially-significant private amenities. Over and over again the impression returned that we were engaged in an exercise of welfare economics in the broader sense of that term.

But other social goals or interests made a bid for attention. The idea of avoiding extremes of power (influence) attracted some support.[5] Critics thought this a case of undue preoccupation with mil-

---

[4] This sharp division does not apply to all conferees. One member, commenting on this report, wanted a third category. He agrees that in principle each should count for one but recognizes the relevance for tax policy of "economies of scale" in family living. Splitting is acceptable to him but on something less than a 50–50 basis.

[5] A conference member said, "I would certainly agree that there is a point at which income splitting at the top of the scale becomes rather inappropriate, in terms of the concept of power. On the other hand, I wonder whether the income tax is the most appropriate means of doing this." Another said:

"The family does have different roles in a society, it seems to me, at different income levels. It is crudely put this way, that at the lowest income level the family is a device for sharing misery. At a high income level it is a device for reducing the tax burden. And at a still higher level it is a way of multiplying influence."

lionaires, of whom there are relatively few. They demanded an answer to the question at what point in the income scale do considerations of power supersede considerations of welfare.[6] The reply was that concern about the redistribution of power is relevant at all income levels and it gradually becomes the main or sole concern as income advances.

Considerable discussion ensued concerning the nature of income distribution and power distribution within the family and whether this should influence tax policy. The fact that the husband is a Democrat or a Republican says nothing about how his wife may cast her vote or her influence. As for more direct factors, such as the choice of consumption patterns, would it be power in decision-making, or benefits (or neither) that should be determining? Do we need further research on how the family typically behaves?[7] Would such research show, for instance, that if the wife works, she has more influence over joint decisions? And would this be of value in tax policy?

Other social goals were defended as relevant: one of them is incentives, particularly for the working wife. One member observed that married women of high economic potential have had (until the 1962 surtax reform) little incentive to work under the mandatory joint return system of Great Britain. If they joined the labor force, it was largely "for the benefit of the Crown." Some thought that consideration should be given to the effect on the birth rate, though this was countered with the view that taxes are not likely to have a major bearing on population trends.

In the later discussion of tax concessions for the aged the view

[6] "In effect, instead of having a positive thesis—that you don't need differentiation for millionaires and you do need it for people on the poverty line he (this author) has in effect a negative thesis—that you don't need differentiation above the poverty line. That isn't obvious to me."

"At my school, there are a number of people who, in recent years, have gotten salaries of $20,000 and even a little better than $20,000 a year. Some of them have six children, and some are childless. It makes a great deal of difference in their standard of living whether they have children going to college or late in high school or not."

[7] The two following comments were made: "The issue I am trying to raise is, do you or don't you want information on what goes on within families, and if you got it, would it make any difference to you."

"I for one would argue that there is no evidence that in any fundamental respect your two sets of families, one in which there is dictatorial control by one member of the family and another where the control is fractionated, so to speak, I can't see intuitively why the two families should pay different taxes, and you're hinging it on this decision."

was expressed that the loss of status which attends a downgrading of income and the absence of opportunity to enlarge one's income by working should not be ignored.

One member offered the opinion that simplicity is an important and much abused canon of taxation and that simple approximations of equity are likely to "wear better" than more elaborate refinements. Perhaps this is but the old problem of whether additional refinements contribute enough to equity to compensate for their administrative complication and their impingement on the revenue. A sentiment frequently expressed at the conference is that we are trying to do too many things with the tax system.

There was some support for the view that earned and property income in the family context are very different species and that the two call for distinct analysis. While for tax purposes earned income is not subject to manipulation within the family by assignment, property income can be divided readily and almost without limit. The simplest of many devices for doing this is by gifts within a family. The point is particularly relevant in the treatment of children's incomes.[8]

Probing for profundity, the conference touched on an ancient philosophical question: whether the concept of "justice" has any meaning independent from social expediency or the serving of social goals. Needless to say, this matter was not fully resolved.

Some thought that in adjusting the tax system to family status more attention should be given to taxes other than the income tax: an expenditures tax, net worth tax, and the death tax. But these participants were reminded that these alternatives are not likely to replace the income tax and that the latter offered quite ample scope for the day's deliberations.

Exemptions

Discussion of exemptions began with the concept of "clear income." Some doubted that it is a useful concept at all,[9] while others

[8] As one member said, "What you are talking about is whether you can carry it (splitting) over to earned income. It is already with us so far as unearned income is concerned and is part of the law being operated on and being used all of the time from day to day."

[9] For example, it was pointed out that "There are all sorts of variations in the requirements of the performance of economic functions of one kind or another and you

felt that it must serve as the basis both for exclusions and graduation. The point was made that our welfare programs are based on some concept of minimal acceptable standards. Some thought that the clear income concept might be avoided by treating exemptions as a tax bracket with a zero rate; others thought that this treatment would be only a formal change in the conception of the problem. The valuable point was made that our welfare system, however imperfect, in some sense adds a bracket below the zero rate, and that in some cases the peculiar feature is added that earnings by the beneficiary may offset subsidies dollar for dollar. This could happen, for instance, when the recipient of aid for dependent children takes a job.

There was considerable interest in the use of tax participation as a means of making people tax conscious and the potency of direct and indirect taxes in this respect.[10]

The conference divided between those who thought the present system of continuing exemptions does not adequately differentiate among families of different size at upper and middle levels of income and those who thought the differentiation is already excessive. Accordingly some favored and some opposed the principle of the tax credit and vanishing exemptions.[11]

One member offered the view that exemption for children is conceptually different from that for adults. Proper policy would require positive children's allowances.[12]

---

have to give expression to all this variety of what has to be subtracted before you hit clear income. . . . If you set aside a certain amount of income as being necessary for minimum efficiency requirements or however you want to call it, and you set this relatively high, and then invade the area with excise taxes or some other kind of taxes, what gain have you made?"

And "I think the average man does have some conception of an income level below which he shouldn't be subject to income taxes."

[10] "I think one of the things that is wrong basically with a great deal of our present system is that there are too many people who take no interest in how public funds are expended, and the reason is that they are not taxed."

"We could do political education more economically and effectively in another way."

[11] For definitions, see Chapter II, pp. 30n, 34–38.

[12] He said, "In the case of treatment of children, I think this is a different matter really altogether. There are incentive problems that have been mentioned. There is the interest of the community as a whole in the welfare of children. It seems to me that the proper way to handle this is not on the basis of equity. The proper way to handle this is by subsidy, which may be declining or not."

The issue was sharpened by a blackboard presentation of differences in family burden by size of family. The purpose of this demonstration in part was to show the wide gap (due to splitting) between single persons and married couples on the one hand and the small difference between the two-spouse family and larger families on the other.[13]

One member argued that if the advisability of more differentiation be conceded, the ideal way to accomplish it would be to allow an exemption as a percentage of income. He supported this proposal on the ground that it affords more freedom (flexibility) than any system of splitting or partial splitting. The proponents of splitting objected on the score that a per capita measure automatically gives the right answers. The discussion illuminated the sharp difference in underlying approach to which previous reference has been made. One member noted that there are political differences in the two approaches.[14]

Obviously for any given taxpayer there is a precise equivalent of the tax value of splitting that could be allowed in terms of a percentage of income allowance. The total tax equals taxable income times an average rate. Thus there is a reduction in base that will exactly compensate for the reduction in rate that is effected by splitting. This author concluded that he should have made more of this type of comparison in the background paper. Whether equivalents could be calculated by a universally applicable formula is a nice problem in mathematics that we shall not attempt to resolve at this point in our project. A fairly simple calculation will show that at the $20,000 level of income, the value of splitting between spouses could be matched in the form of an additional exemption of approximately 16 percent of joint income. (The calculation assumes that the present standard deduction is taken.) The saving on a $3,200 reduction in the tax base compensates for the $1,568 saving that arises from the reduced rates applicable under splitting.

Little attention was given to the significance of marginal, as

---

[13] "It is the wife, you see, who gives an enormous advantage, and then the differences by family size are relatively small. Perhaps there is too much concession for the spouse and not enough for the children."

[14] He said, "I don't think you could ever get through Congress the kind of exemption system that would approximate a per capita split, but you might get a per capita split through Congress."

opposed to effective, rates though one member volunteered the view
that the objective of reducing marginal rates by means of vanishing
exemptions is principally one of "obfuscation."[15]

Not much attention could be afforded either to the interesting
question of the relation of deductions to exemptions. Here it was
noted that the President's proposal in 1963 to allow a minimum
standard deduction was in some aspects much like a vanishing
exemption. The thought was added that this device introduced a
new degree of freedom into the tax mechanism.

Considerable attention was given at the conference to the application of the exemption system to students over 19 years of age.
Some critics accepted a view introduced in the background paper
that present allowances are in conflict with vertical equity.[16] They
preferred that exemptions be cut off at a specified age, eliminating
the special student category entirely. Other critics agreed that the
student exemption is a questionable means of promoting education
and sought some discussion of whether and how students should be
allowed to write off the capital invested in their training. The point
was made that education is a form of investment that the public
might want to encourage, and while it may do this by providing free
facilities, that method may be inadequate in the case of some individuals. It was noted that the problem is related to that of the aggregation of family income in general, including the income of minors,
and to the fact that minors with income usually involve a double
exemption limited only by the support test.[17]

Considerable support was expressed for the Canadian rule
which, with qualifications, aggregates the property income of minors with that of parents.[18] As to earned income, it was noted that

[15] As he stated, "Maybe it is a good thing to disguise the marginal rate in this con-
nection, but I am all in favor of laying the cards on the table and having everything
above board. This is Machiavellian to me."

[16] For example, one said, "It seems to me giving an exemption based on the student
state—upon the fact that a person between 18 and 21, say, is a student—is almost
exactly the reverse of what equity would indicate is proper. It benefits those who are
primarily in high income groups and those who are most likely to be able to earn a
relatively large sum later in their lives."

[17] "It is the double exemption for those under the age of 18 that is by all odds the
more important one. The student aspect is a sort of continuation of that."

[18] One participant said, "And this game is now being played for unearned income
as a means of getting $600 of unearned income to the minor tax free. In fact, what you

often this is spent by the youth on his own account and makes only a scant contribution toward easing the parent's budget.

Two solutions were suggested: One would leave the law as it is except that the parent to claim a minor as a dependent must include all of the latter's unearned income. The other would allow minors and students an additional $300 or $400 for earned income. Thus these junior workers would pay tax only if they earned $900 or $1,000. To claim these people as dependents, parents would have to aggregate dependents' incomes with their own. This practice would usually be unprofitable. (The discussion left somewhat ambiguous the question whether, if a double exemption is claimed, all income of the minor or student must be aggregated or only the excess above the present exemption.) It appeared that the suggestion was a cross between Professor Harriss' proposal (see pp. 42–43) and one made by this author, namely to allow a double exemption for the working student.[19] The inequities associated with the exemption of scholarships got little attention.

Special Concessions for the Aged

Discussion of tax privileges for the aged focused on two questions: (1) Is it appropriate to use the income tax system as a vehicle for improving the lot of the aged? and (2) Should social security benefits be taxed, and if so, how?

As to the first question, strong support was indicated for the author's view expressed in the background paper that the income tax system is a crude and unhappy means for mitigating the lot of old people. It cannot do so without giving unwanted favors to the

---

do is that you set up a trust and you distribute out of the trust each year up to $600 to the minor. You keep the rest of the income in trust. And you have two tax entities. The trust itself has an exemption of $100. So you really get an exemption of $700 for unearned income of a minor."

[19] However there was objection to the latter suggestion: "I just wanted to say that I don't like to see tax provisions that push the student or the young person in one way or the other, that will make his family encourage him to stop working, as the old system did, as he approached $600; or other systems such as the one outlined in Professor Groves' paper that would suggest that they should be encouraged to work, that they'd get an exemption if they did. I would like to see some arrangement that would be neutral as far as the child's working is concerned."

wealthy aged; it cannot help the most needy among the senior citizens; and it develops inequities among the aged themselves. Half of all persons aged sixty-five and older still have annual cash incomes of less than $1,000. There are programs that would undoubtedly provide more generously for these people, but they lie outside the tax system and cannot be helped by it.

Some dissent to this view, as previously indicated, stressed the special circumstances of the aged: their loss of status because of retirement; their lack of opportunity to augment meager income with earnings; their disappointed expectations because of inflation. Here it was argued that the general present personal exemption allowances are admittedly inadequate but tolerated because most people earn or can earn more than the exclusion. Dissenters suggested that none of these special considerations applied exclusively to older people. It was agreed at least that special income tax favors for the aged should be granted, if at all, in such manner as to exclude the wealthy contingent of that class.

Older people probably also have some built-in advantages under the general provisions of the income tax law. Not only are their consumption needs as indicated by budget studies somewhat less than those of younger taxpayers; their budgets stress shelter and medical care, both of which are favorably treated under the law. Imputed income from owner-occupied shelter is not taxed; property taxes are a deductible item; and medical care is allowed as an expense with qualifications. The conference noted that it is probably property taxes that provide the most onerous tax pinch for many of the elderly and observed that a movement to provide special homestead exemptions for the aged at the state and local levels had gathered considerable momentum. Whether this would afford a better fit in adjusting taxes to the needs of older people remained to be seen, but it appeared to have a plausible claim to being a more rational approach.

Little if any dissent greeted the proposal that social security benefits should be taxed. It was noted that the contrary provision in federal taxation is an historical accident. One member quite familiar with the field observed that the tax exemption of OASDI benefits, particularly as applied to rich recipients, acts as a brake on the liberalization of the program. Accordingly there was wide agreement that at least employers' contributions and the element of interest on accumulations should somehow be subject to tax.

The consensus disappeared, however, when the conference turned to the question of how the transition to taxability should be accomplished. One group argued for treating social security benefits like private pensions: ascertaining at retirement total employee contributions and excluding this portion from taxation over the years as the benefits were received. Another group objected to this, some on the ground that it would be difficult and cumbersome to administer, others on the ground that it runs contrary to the spirit of social security, which eschews the actuarial calculus. The fact emerged that the Social Security Administration does not currently have information on the total contributions of its covered workers though such totals could be approximated from data on taxable earnings.[20] At present these contributions are, in the aggregate, a minor though not negligible, part of receipts. Social security as presently financed operates on the principle that the working population supports the elderly and that the former will be supported by a new generation of workers in due time. Among other things this accounts for the fact that a program to permit deduction of current contributions and tax benefits would affect the revenue negatively. Some arbitrary division of current benefits into a taxable and nontaxable portion was suggested. It could be based on the general experience with regard to contributions by employers, employees, and interest.

None of this, however, appealed to those who preferred straight annuity treatment; they argued that this is the only sound and neutral procedure, the one that is best for the revenue, and one that is by no means beyond the range of administrative possibility.

[20] One member warned, "As long as people are figuring out fancy systems, they might as well know that the Social Security Administration does not have a record of contributions. It has a record of earnings, and this is rather different, in terms of this business of calculating during month so and so the contributions that should have been made on this . . . were at this rate, then at another rate and so forth.

"So if you want to count the administrative cost, it's fantastically greater than you think it is."

Splitting

Intensive discussion of the subject of splitting was introduced with information concerning recent developments abroad presented by one of the members. There has been considerable agitation in several countries for per capita treatment of income, fostered mostly by women's organizations. In Germany the movement has been aided and abetted by the courts. They held invalid the aggregation of incomes earned independently by two spouses. This led to legislation providing for splitting—which is itself a form of aggregation and a somewhat anomalous sequel to the court's decision. Austria and Ceylon have also adopted splitting, the latter extending the system to include children, as in France. Agitation for legislation of this sort has been strong in Japan but is being vigorously resisted by the government. It was noted that, with or without splitting, some concessions to working wives are a widespread phenomenon.

The Ceylon system is particularly interesting; it divides income among members of the family (and others) for tax purposes as follows:

Single person (bachelor, spinster, widow or widower)	$1\frac{1}{2}$ units
Married man	$1\frac{1}{2}$ units
Wife	$\frac{1}{2}$ unit
Child	$\frac{1}{2}$ unit
Dependent relative	$\frac{1}{2}$ unit

The maximum number of parts or units applicable to a family is limited to four. Thus in the common case of two spouses and two children with an aggregate income, let us say, of $10,000, half, or $5,000 would be attributable to the male spouse and the other half divided equally among the female spouse and the two children— $1,666 each. This modified quotient system is said to be based in part on the problem of gifts to minors and dependents. It would appear to compromise considerably with the idea that each shall count for one and only one.[21]

---

[21] The member also explained the "highly regarded" Swedish dual-rate system, noting that it uses a double-width bracket for married couples at the bottom of the scale. This gives an end effect, disregarding the special allowance for working wives, exactly like our splitting. After the first bracket, however, the bracket widths are the same, and this keeps the rates for married couples *slightly* lower than those for single

Nearly everyone at the conference favored pooling family income for tax purposes, but one member stood staunchly for a return of the pre-1948 system, with qualifications. However, this consensus settled very little; the real issue concerns the relative amounts of taxes which single and family taxpayers should pay.

To sharpen the issue, the chairman presented in the following form what seemed to him to be the author's views: Given a common (and modest) aggregate taxable income, the two-job family should be taxed less than the one-job family, and both should be taxed (somewhat) less than a single person. This presentation left aside the quantitative aspect (degree of distinction), the further problem of children, and the personal exemptions and deductions. The chairman's hope that this might precipitate a definite consensus was not realized. Some thought that the model was oversimplified and that it must be expanded to include variations in size of income and alternatives with unearned income. The proposition that there should be concessions to the working wife led to a prolonged discussion concerning imputed incomes (including the value of leisure); relative home and work expenses of working and nonworking wives; and the question whether economies in family arrangements should have any bearing on tax liabilities. The conference was reminded that decisions in this area hinge heavily on the philosophical criteria discussed earlier.

The discussion highlighted one of the questions of fact that might bear on the argument. We do not have any very precise knowledge of the "economies of scale" that attend family living. We do have budget studies indicating that at modest levels of income two married people can "live as well" as a single person when the former have aggregate income about 1.4 times the latter. In other words, two married people with an aggregate income of $7,000 can live as well as a single person with $5,000. But we do not know the degree to which the scale would vary between the two-job family and the one-job family, and we do not know whether the so-called

---

people. At a high level of income, differentiation ceases entirely. However, in the Netherlands, differentials are maintained throughout the scale sometimes being as much as 50 percent higher for single persons than for married couples with the same aggregate taxable incomes.

economies of scale are an increasing or decreasing function of rising income. One member volunteered the conviction that his "welfare function" would not improve substantially were his wife to drop out of the picture. When a bachelor takes on a spouse, the food and clothing required might approximately double, but the same would not be true of the television set or perhaps the automobile or bill for entertainment. The addition of a child to a well-to-do family, at least in the early years of the child's life, could hardly reduce the family's potential scale of living by as much as one-third. Here we have an area where research might supply a positive solution to what appears to be a strictly normative problem. However, it would not be easy to judge the cut in welfare potential in the upper income ranges that follows marriage or the enlargement of a family. And as previously observed, there are those who apparently do not accept a comparative welfare criterion as evidence bearing on the issue. This criterion departs from the idea that each should always count for one and no more than one.

Some attention was given to the ubiquitous nature of sharing; that it occurs both within the immediate family and to some extent outside of it. Note was taken of the fact that even the bachelor shares more or less with his "dates." The law now recognizes this broader area of sharing, both in its provision for dependents' exemptions and in its provision for partial splitting in the case of so-called "householders." However, no attempt was made at the conference to determine how the lines that recognize partial sharing might be drawn more rationally.

A final note was sounded, namely that if there were to be politically acceptable changes in the existing law, they would probably take the form of modest mitigation of the "unconscionable" tax burdens now cast upon single taxpayers. Not much sympathy was to be expected for bachelors and spinsters; according to code they shirk the responsibilities which families shoulder. The point was made that many single people are elderly widows and widowers, of whom no such criticisms can be made. Some sympathy was expressed for the view that a married person should not face increased taxes merely because his spouse has died. But this returned the conference to its fundamental cleavage, the per capita school contending that this was analogous to the dissolution of a partnership, leaving fewer partners to share a constant aggregate income.

For a summary of the conference's views on splitting, the reader is referred to the introduction to this chapter. Indeed it was the issue of splitting that exposed the sharp cleavage on the tax significance of the family. The group that views the family's income as an aggregate to be divided by the number of members of course favored splitting. The group that regards the addition of a spouse or a child as a minor dilution of a pre-existing status of welfare and power (adequately respected by an exemption allowance) opposed it.

Conclusion

In addition to underlining the fundamental differences between two schools of thought concerning the proper role of progressive income taxation in relation to family situations, the conference developed the following provocative ideas:

1. That not only may comparative welfare vary with family status but the variation itself may be a function of the size of family income. (Not only can two people "live cheaper than one" [per capita], but two people with an income of $100,000 can live better than one person with the same income—to a greater degree than is the case at lower income levels.) A need for more research was indicated here.

2. That further differentiation by family size in the upper and middle income ranges (if desired) might easily be accomplished by an exemption in terms of a percentage of income.

3. That the taxation of social security benefits might provide an exclusion based on the general, rather than the specific, experience of taxpayers. (Thus if 20 percent of social security benefits represent a return of previously taxed contributions *on the average*, 80 percent of these benefits would be considered taxable income.)

4. That government welfare programs with their system of subsidies can and should be conceived as in some sense supplementing the tax system and providing a sub-zero bracket of rates.

5. That the proper tax treatment of working wives is a problem in some degree separable from that of wives generally under the in-

come tax. This problem will have to be faced whether or not splitting continues and is a subject that invites empirical research.

6. That at least for some people further information on how income distribution and/or decision-making typically occur within
the family would illuminate the problem significantly.

The conference served to underline the author's contention in
the introduction to this book that a rational solution to the subtle
tax problems in our assigned area must begin with a thorough
examination of fundamental criteria. Discussion that does not take
account of these fundamentals cannot define real differences and
areas of agreement.

List of Conference Participants

Martin Atlas
The Cafritz Company

Walter J. Blum
Professor of Law
University of Chicago

Harvey E. Brazer
Professor of Economics
University of Michigan

James M. Buchanan
Professor of Economics
University of Viriginia

Eveline Burns
Professor of Economics
New York School of Social Work
Columbia University

Robert D. Calkins
President
The Brookings Institution

James Casner
Professor of Law
Harvard University

L. Laszlo Ecker-Racz
Assistant Director
Advisory Commission on Inter-
governmental Relations

Richard Goode
The Brookings Institution

Marion Gillim
Professor of Economics
Barnard College

Harold M. Groves
Professor of Economics
University of Wisconsin

Daniel Holland
Professor of Economics
School of Industrial Management
Massachusetts Institute of Tech-
nology

C. Harry Kahn
Professor of Economics
Rutgers University

Robert Lampman
Professor of Economics
University of Wisconsin

Ida Merriam
Director
Research and Statistics Division
Social Security Administration

Oliver Oldman
Professor of Law
Harvard University

Joseph A. Pechman
Director of Economic Studies
The Brookings Institution

Melvin Reder
Professor of Economics
Stanford University

Alice M. Rivlin
The Brookings Institution

Earl Rolph
Professor of Economics
University of California

Harry Rudick
Lord, Day, and Lord

Lawrence Seltzer
Professor of Economics
Wayne State University

Conference Participants (*Continued*)

Louis Shere
  Professor of Economics
  Indiana University

Carl S. Shoup
  Professor of Economics
  Columbia University

Stanley S. Surrey
  Assistant Secretary
  U. S. Treasury Department

Norman B. Ture
  Director of Tax Research
  National Bureau of Economic
  Research, Inc.

William Vickrey
  Professor of Economics
  Columbia University

Index